The Ultimate Guide to

Chick Flicks

Introduction

Admit it. After catching the latest fashion/fantasy chick flick at the local multiplex, you've rushed home to try on your prettiest dress in the hope of making your life more like the glitzy existence portrayed on the silver screen. We all have. Chick flicks have such power that we are hesitant to reveal how much we are affected. Publicly, we may pretend we're immune. Privately, we enjoy nothing more than a good cinematic shopping montage and a happy ending. There's a reason Julia Roberts's movies have racked up over $2.5 billion worldwide. We're helpless to resist. How can we? By definition, these films are specifically created to appeal to females—our emotions, our issues, our fantasies, our fears. That's why we can watch them over and over and over again and never tire of them. Although chick flicks can run the gamut from sunny Disney movies to melodramatic tearjerkers, one of the most popular themes is that true love will prevail despite all obstacles. Who doesn't want to believe that?

Chick flicks are sassy and full of fun. If you go to the movies hoping to see a great makeover scene, at least one red-hot make out session, and a finale consisting of an elaborate public declaration of love, a chick flick is definitely the ticket. If the filmmakers throw in a scene of a man washing a woman's hair (especially if the man is young Robert Redford in *Out of Africa*), we'll wear out our copy of the DVD. Don't get me wrong, we chick flick aficionados also enjoy movies with lots of explosions and people running around with guns drawn. We even like foreign films (especially those set in Paris). But what makes us really melt is when girls with great hair triumph over adversity and hunky bad boys get domesticated. Say it loud and say it proud: I love chick flicks!

Chick flick enthusiasts don't just sit back and watch the movies. We actively try to import a little bit of the romance, glamour, and old-fashioned Hollywood magic into our own lives. After all, where is it written that life can't imitate art? It can—and should.

The term "chick flicks" rubs some people the wrong way. Amy Pascal, chairman of Columbia Pictures, remarked when accepting the Women in Film 2001 Crystal Award, "It has been said that I make chick flicks. This is not a compliment." Mike Newell, the British director who gave us such A+ chick flicks as *Four Weddings and a Funeral* and *Mona Lisa Smile*, also protests, "I don't like the term. I think it denigrates a movie. It has overtones of talking down to women, like they are second best. We don't call *The Last Samurai* a [guy] flick, do we?"

What's the difference between "guy flicks" and "chick flicks"? The former feature boys and their toys, the latter girls and their curls. Chick flicks are the equivalent of *Vogue, Marie Claire*, and *Lucky*—magazines clearly targeted to a feminine demographic and of very little interest to those with testosterone; however, they are in no way inferior to (in fact, are arguably superior to) *GQ, Maxim*, or *Cargo*.

Longtime chick flick enthusiasts don't need to be informed that for decades so-called women's pictures have won Best Picture at the Academy Awards: *Chicago* (2002), *Shakespeare in Love* (1998), *The English Patient*

(1996), *Driving Miss Daisy* (1989), *Out of Africa* (1985), *Terms of Endearment* (1983), *Ordinary People* (1980), *Kramer vs. Kramer* (1979), *Annie Hall* (1977), *The Sound of Music* (1965), *My Fair Lady* (1964), *West Side Story* (1961), *Gigi* (1958), *All About Eve* (1950), *Casablanca* (1943), *Mrs. Miniver* (1942), *How Green Was My Valley* (1941), *Rebecca* (1940), *Gone with the Wind* (1939), *It Happened One Night* (1934), and *Grand Hotel* (1931). All Oscar winners, all what we in the modern era call chick flicks.

Chick flicks also rule at the box office. The second most successful independent film of all time? *My Big Fat Greek Wedding*, grossing $241 million at the U.S. box office, beaten only by Mel Gibson's *The Passion of the Christ*. The biggest box office grosser of 1990? *Pretty Woman*.

This guide is not a comprehensive review of every chick flick ever made. Hollywood keeps making new ones (thank Heaven!), so a complete accounting would be impossible. Although the main emphasis is on motion pictures* produced in the decades following Julia Roberts's birth, we'll look at plenty of older favorites too. While some may be unfamiliar to you, almost all should be available at your local video store and many are probably already in your personal library. After all, is there anyone alive who hasn't seen *Pretty Woman*? Even Romy and Michele have, and they're fictional characters in a chick flick.†

This handbook begins by examining the essential elements that go into making a chick flick—from original inspiration to the casting of a quintessential chick flick superstar. The focus then shifts to individual films—from the most beloved to the relatively obscure—culminating in a calendar plan for a full year of chick flick viewing. That leads us to good parts—the sexiest, most glamorous, and ultimately tearjerking moments ever captured on film. Finally, because chick flick fans always want more,

---

*And made-for-television flicks released on home video
†*Romy and Michele's High School Reunion* (1997)

we conclude with discussion points, a pop quiz, and a cornucopia of personal recommendations from fellow chick flick enthusiasts.

Load up on champagne, strawberries, and dental floss, dear readers, then plop your *Pretty Woman* DVD in the player and indulge. If your husband's lucky, he'll return home to a romantic bubble bath for two. After all, we don't just watch chick flicks, we live them.

From Meeting Cute to the Ultimate Happy Ending

How to Create the Perfect Romance

S o what exactly is a chick flick? Perhaps the classic definition of pornography applies: we know it when we see it. (Not to imply in any way that chick flicks are pornography, though I do have a friend who calls Sandra Bullock's *Hope Floats* "porn for girls.") A more concrete definition might be a movie that specifically appeals to viewers with a feminine sensibility.

Quite often the stars, story line, and marketing campaign make it immediately obvious whether something falls in the chick flick camp or not. Male teenagers, in particular, seem to have an infallible radar detector warning them away from a film that their mother might enjoy, while female teenagers innately sense that anything with "wedding" or "princess" in the title is worthy of their patronage.

Most chick flicks aren't concerned with winning the male audience over. The films might feature car chases and explosions (typical guy flick modus operandi), but those chases and explosions are employed in pursuit of the most important thing of all: love. Why are chick flick enthusiasts so fascinated by the twists and turns of love? "Love is the ultimate magic," theorizes *Practical Magic* writer Alice Hoffman, "the ultimate goal with no reason, often making no sense. We spend our lives trying to make those kind of things practical—why do I love him, why does he love me. Basically, it's just magic." Nothing captures and displays that magic better than a chick flick.

Incorporating everything from epic costume dramas to old-fashioned Hollywood musicals to family-friendly fables to contemporary working girl comedies, the chick flick genre is too broad to analyze as a whole. Nevertheless, an examination of the fundamental ingredients in a chick flick romance reveals a prototypical pattern that can be broken down into ten basic steps.

Step One: Create a Sympathetic Heroine

Even if the female lead is a prostitute or the Queen of England, she should be saddled with a plight not so removed from the viewer's own life. The heroine needs to be a character whom everyone in the audience— from a teenage bookworm secretly in love with the big man on campus to an over-worked at the office/under-appreciated at home C.E.O.—can relate to. The actresses playing these heroines don't seem too far removed from the girl next door, which is why we deem them to be mega-love-worthy and embrace them as America's sweethearts. Consequently, Renée Zellweger can play a socially inept neurotic in *Bridget Jones's Diary* and a cold-blooded murderess in *Chicago* and still have the audience rooting for her. Inaccessibly beautiful actresses are usually cast as the villains, the "bad girlfriends" whom the male leads are superficially attracted to before realizing their mistake. "Invariably the 'third character' part in a romantic comedy is a bitch or an ice princess or really unlikable," agrees Alicia Witt, who played Sandra Bullock's rival for Hugh Grant's affection in *Two Weeks Notice*.

Step Two: Offer up a Love-Worthy Hero

Of course, the heroine doesn't realize how loveable the hero is at first— if they were a perfect match from the start, there wouldn't be any story to tell, would there? Because he'll change over the course of the movie, the hero is often flawed at the start. To compensate for this handicap, the actor has to use his personal charm and charisma to infuse likeability into the role. Analyzing Dennis Quaid and his character in *Something to Talk About*, producer Paula Weinstein comments, "Dennis made Eddie, who after all, has been stepping out on his wife, an immensely compassionate and complicated human being." Tom Hanks is also good at playing a cad worthy of redemption. "Tom has such charm," proclaims *You've Got Mail* director Nora Ephron, "he is so irresistible that he can play a bad guy and you never once believe that he doesn't truly have a heart."

Love at first sight can occur. However, this instant love connection is tested by a series of bumps in the hero and heroine's relationship. To permanently win the affection of his true love, the hero must make a grand gesture, a public declaration of everlasting love. But wait, we're getting ahead of ourselves . . .

Step Three: Don't Forget the Best Friend

If the heroine needs to explain her feelings to someone, or perhaps she requires additional motivation to do the right thing, she should come equipped with a best friend. Because this character often provides comic relief and can't be perceived as a potential rival for the hero's affection, the best friend role is usually cast with quirky comediennes or gay men. Whoopi Goldberg is an excellent instigator in *How Stella Got Her Groove Back*, Rosie O'Donnell provides a similar nudge in *Sleepless in Seattle*, and Rupert Everett proves to be Julia Roberts's ultimate champion in *My Best Friend's Wedding*. The hero, by the way, often has his own Sancho Panza, usually a coworker. But unlike their female counterpart, the male best friend sometimes poaches. Think Jason Alexander in *Pretty Woman*.

Step Four: Something's Wrong with the Heroine's Life

Sometimes our girl isn't fulfilled at work. Or she hungers for a family. In the Britney Spears vehicle, *Crossroads*, the teenage heroine (Lucy) has mother-abandonment issues. "We all have certain questions in life, and Lucy's is finding her mother," explains Kim Cattrall, who plays the AWOL matriarch. "Once she does, she can put that to rest and get on with her life, as opposed to always being connected to this phantom figure."

The heroine feels incomplete because she has not yet achieved her destiny. While in limbo, she can fall victim to Bad Boyfriend Syndrome. Bad boyfriends are not to be confused with bad boys. A bad boy is a beast who just needs a little tender loving care from a beauty before he can be recognized as a true prince. A bad boyfriend, on the other hand, might be a prince, but he's not the heroine's true destiny.

Meg Ryan has Bad Boyfriend Syndrome in *Sleepless in Seattle*. "Walter represents the perfect man to take home to your family," the actress says of her character's initial wrong choice in potential mates. "He's wonderful, but something is wrong with the relationship, and Annie doesn't know herself well enough to know what she really wants."

What's worse than having a bad boyfriend? Having no boyfriend! Renée Zellweger's problem in *Bridget Jones's Diary* is written in capital letters on the DVD cover—she's UNMARRIED. Director Sharon Maguire can relate to her heroine's plight. "I know the world so well because it's mine. We were having a really good time, going out partying, and we didn't really want that to stop. At the same time, we were anxious why we hadn't settled down yet. Yet, we thought we shouldn't be striving for male approval anyway because we were feminists. That contradiction is the thing that [writer] Helen [Fielding] so brilliantly captured in *Bridget Jones's Diary*. There are a lot of women out there who've got their careers, their independence—but they're constantly thinking, 'I just want to be in love. I just want a man.'"

Step Five: They Meet

Unless the chick flick is a tearjerker, our heroine and her true love are guaranteed to end up together in the final reel. But first they have to meet, usually in a memorable way—or better yet, a "cute" way. In *The Wedding Planner*, Matthew McConaughey saves Jennifer Lopez from a runaway garbage bin. "They have this kind of chance meeting," J.Lo explains. "It's a big accident, and then they get thrown together for the rest of the day. She definitely feels something right away, and it's something she hasn't felt in a long time. It takes her by surprise. She really doesn't know what to make of it, but it's exciting."

"I think the most incredible thing about love is the actual moment when the two people find each other," agrees Drew Barrymore, who starred with Adam Sandler in another wedding-themed flick. "In *The Wedding Singer*, they literally find each other over a kid throwing up. It just doesn't get much more romantic than that!"

Step Six: Toss in Impediments to the Romance

"The trap in making romantic comedy today," complains Neal Moritz, who produced the Reese Witherspoon vehicle *Sweet Home Alabama*, "is that audiences feel like they've seen everything that can happen already—the boy and girl are going to get together in the end. So, in order to avoid these clichés, we've tried to put in a number of twists and turns, to give the audience a movie they haven't seen before. They won't have the feeling that they know the end of the movie before it begins."

Whether it's a deadly disease, a bet, a workplace rivalry, or a romantic triangle, the best impediments have high stakes and provide a real challenge to the characters' love. It's in this "complications ensue" stage that so many chick flicks founder. Even with a tearjerker like *Sweet No-vember*, the audience must feel invested in events prior to Charlize Theron's swan song. *Sweet November* director, Pat O'Connor, recalls, "I tried to make this film bounce along with a certain gusto and panache and style." To do that, he relied on "the delight in the challenge of the unexpected." Could he be referring to Charlize's transvestite neighbor?

Step Seven: They Dance

Waltzes and tangos aren't included in chick flicks just to spoon-feed the audience big screen images of their fondest desires (in real life, most chicks love to shake their tail feathers while most guys would chew off their own leg rather than shake it on the dance floor). Dancing also cin-ematically illustrates that the heroine and hero are destined for each other. "We think of it as the ultimate symbol of romance," explains *The Wedding Planner* screenwriters Michael Ellis and Pamela Falk, "because it's the closest two people can come without kissing or actual sex. It's foreplay. It's a symbol of a connection without saying anything."

Step Eight: Pack in as Many Memorable Moments as Possible

Although every plot is different, every successful motion picture delivers a sufficient number of wows to leave the audience feeling satisfied. In guy flicks, explosions and car chases are the money shots. Chick flicks must deliver their equivalent big bangs—those "awwwwww" and "I wish that were meeeeeeee!" bits—to make viewers eager to watch the film again. Who can forget Daniel Day-Lewis's waterfall promise to come back to Madeline Stowe in *The Last of the Mohicans*? Or *The Witches of Eastwick* trio (Cher, Michelle Pfeiffer, and Susan Sarandon) literally flying around the balloon-filled ballroom? Or Angela Bassett in *Waiting to Exhale*, loading her philandering husband's expensive suits into his sports car and torching it? These scenes alone are worth the price of admission. They're also the reason why DVDs are God's gift to movie fans—it's so easy to go straight to the good parts.

Step Nine: The Hero Employs
the Three Magic Words

Chick flicks serve up on a beautifully garnished platter another thing we desperately wish real men would do as willingly as their fictional counterparts: say "I love you." In movies packed with A+ moments, the hero typically has to overcome major obstacles to pronounce the Three Magic Words at just the right time, in an extremely public situation. And because he has the benefit of a hardworking screenwriter putting carefully crafted phrases in his mouth, a hero like Jerry Maguire will utter those heartfelt words more memorably than any average joe ever could.

Step Ten: Achieve the Ultimate Happy (or unhappy) Ending

In *The Philadelphia Story*, Katherine Hepburn and Cary Grant get hitched (for the second time) moments before the credits roll. Traditionally, the exchange of vows symbolizes that the heroine and hero's courtship story line has concluded satisfactorily. Recent chick flicks have offered viewers an international buffet of I Dos: *Monsoon Wedding* (2001), *Muriel's Wedding* (1994), *My Big Fat Greek Wedding* (2002), *Polish Wedding* (1998), and the binge-worthy *Four Weddings and a Funeral* (1994). However, even if there is a marriage ceremony in a movie, the viewer is not necessarily guaranteed a happy ending—because a seemingly happy-go-lucky chick flick can take an unexpected turn and reveal itself to be a tearjerker (as *Steel Magnolias* fans well know).

If you're smiling or crying as the credits roll, your viewing experience can be judged a success. You'll feel like Yul Brynner, who after whirling Deborah Kerr around the palace floor in *The King and I*, proclaims, "Again!" Yul finds things to be just as glorious the second time around, and you will too. When it comes to enjoying a chick flick romance, repeat as many times as necessary.

CHAPTER 2

Wishful Thinking

Why Motion Pictures Are Like Real Life—but Better

s there anything more enchanting than Audrey Hepburn taking a break from her royal duties to explore Rome with Gregory Peck in *Roman Holiday*? How fun is it to be Drew Barrymore, ditching her boring grown-up job as a newspaper copyeditor to go undercover as a hip high school student in *Never Been Kissed*? Who doesn't want to tag along with Susan Sarandon as she packs up her T-bird for a carefree weekend fishing trip with Geena Davis in *Thelma & Louise*? One of the reasons why we watch chick flicks is to indulge in a vicarious thrill as characters we identify with leave their mundane existence behind and embark on a potentially excellent adventure.

While there is an undeniable element of escapism, cinematic story lines are often inspired by real-life experiences. Let's examine the many ways a kernel of reality can be buffed, shined, and glamorized by screenwriters until it's worthy of becoming a chick flick fantasy.

A Historical Event Becomes a Backdrop for a Fictional Romance

CASE STUDY: TITANIC (1997)

Writer/director James Cameron knew he had the technology to recreate the dramatic sinking of the famous ocean liner. What he needed were characters the audience would root for, even though, as Cameron points out, "Every single moment that you're with them, there is this little voice in the back of your mind that says they're all doomed." He created a fictional pair of star-crossed lovers, poor boy Jack (played by Leonardo DiCaprio) and wealthy debutante Rose (Kate Winslet). While Winslet proclaims, "I believe this story does take you to the point where you would do anything you could to stop that ship from sinking in order for Rose and Jack to be together," screenwriter Cameron emphasizes the reality of the situation. "We wanted to tell a fictional story within absolutely rigorous, historically accurate terms," he stresses. "All the accuracy and all the special visual effects are intended for one purpose: to put viewers on *Titanic*. It's a very you-are-there kind of experience." Thus DVD viewers can survive history's ultimate shipwreck in the safety of their own home whenever they so desire.

The Autobiographical Experience Gets Glamorized

CASE STUDY: HOW STELLA GOT HER GROOVE BACK (1998)

In real life, novelist Terry McMillan made a spur-of-the-moment trip to Jamaica after a particularly tough period in her life in which she lost her mother and best friend. While on the island, she fell in love with a much younger man. Twenty years younger. McMillan created the fictional Stella and the story of how she reinvigorated her life by falling in love with a Jamaican two decades her junior "in essence but not in particular" to her own experience. First she wrote the book, then the movie, in which Angela Bassett plays not a novelist but a stockbroker feeling at loose ends when her son goes off to stay with her ex-husband. A "Come to Jamaica" commercial on TV inspires her to call up her best friend, Whoopi Goldberg, and head down to the island for some R&R. There she meets a young stud named Winston Shakespeare, played by the impossibly handsome Taye Diggs. Both the novel and the movie are wonderful, although the movie has the advantage of showcasing Taye sans shirt. If Terry McMillan's real-life Romeo is half as good looking, it's no wonder she brought him back to the States with her.

Real People Become Fictionalized

CASE STUDY: ROMY AND MICHELE'S HIGH SCHOOL REUNION (1997)

Chick flick creators can find inspiration anywhere. "I was standing in the restroom and couldn't help listening to these two incredible women talking," recalls writer Robin Schiff. "They went on and on, for almost ten minutes, saying things like, 'God, I love your hair!' which prompted the other to say, 'My hair? You like my hair? I'll give you my hair!' It was so banal that inadvertently it became the most entertaining and perhaps most frightening conversation I'd ever heard." The airheads first became supporting characters in a play called *Ladies Room*, and then were brought to the big screen as leading ladies in full glory. In the movie version, the two ditzy blondes, played by Mira Sorvino and Lisa Kudrow, are given an agenda: go to their high school reunion. "I had to add further dimension to these two women, and work to develop them and their stories into an interesting movie," admits Schiff.

A Career Becomes More Extreme

CASE STUDY: THE WEDDING PLANNER (2001)

The idea for *The Wedding Planner* leaped out at screenwriters Pamela Falk and Michael Ellis when they were idly flipping through a Learning Annex catalogue and spotted a class entitled "How to Be a Wedding Planner." "We thought: What kind of person plans other people's weddings? We thought it would be a funny juxtaposition to have a wedding planner with a nonexistent love life." They then met with wedding planners. "What we found out was that it's a world that's very far from romance and love. We had lunch with one wedding planner who told us that she didn't even believe in marriage. So we took that to the next level in the script, where [Jennifer Lopez's character] Mary is not only unsentimental about the weddings she plans, but has them down to a science. She can actually tell how long a couple will stay together by the different choices they make for their wedding song or the color of the bridesmaids' dresses."

A Missed Opportunity Is Taken

CASE STUDY: THE FAVOR (1994)

The advertising line for *The Favor* reads, "Two Women, Three Men, One Secret." Harley Jane Kozak and Elizabeth McGovern play best friends, the former married to Bill Pullman, the latter dating Brad Pitt. Once again a high school reunion becomes a catalyst as the married pal asks her single friend to do her one small favor: look up old boyfriend, Ken Wahl. The concept driving *The Favor* was inspired by Hollywood screenwriter Sara Parriott's trip home to Finley, Ohio, for her high school reunion. "Please look up my old boyfriend for me," her writing partner, Josann McGibbon, requested. Admitting she still had occasional dreams about him, McGibbon remembers she begged Parriott, "'I'm married. I've got kids. If you could just sort of check him out, it would possibly put an end to my fantasies.' And then we discussed what would happen if she slept with him and then told me it was fabulous."

An Idle Fantasy Is Explored

CASE STUDY: NOTTING HILL (1999)

In *Notting Hill*, Julia Roberts plays a Julia Roberts–like megastar who wanders into Hugh Grant's bookshop and ends up dating him. The screenwriter Richard Curtis stumbled across his concept during a bout of insomnia. "When I was lying sleepless at night, I would sometimes wonder what it would be like if I just turned up at my friends' house, where I used to have dinner once a week, with the most famous person at that time, be it Madonna or Princess Diana. It all sprang from there. How would my friends react—who would try to be cool? How would you get through dinner? What would they say to you afterward? That was the starting point, the idea of a very normal person going out with an unbelievably famous person and how that impinges on their lives."

How realistic is the resulting romantic comedy? Julia Roberts demurs, "People will just assume that because I am playing an actor in this movie that she is me, or that I understand everything about her life—I don't. Every actor's experience is different." Having said that, she adds, "I have often said that people's perception of my life or an actor's life is a lot more hectic and outrageous and pressure-filled and glamorous than I have ever known my life to be, or the life of any of my actor friends."

An Everyday Situation Is Exaggerated

CASE STUDY: ONE FINE DAY (1996)

As the title suggests, all the action in *One Fine Day* takes place in a twenty-four-hour period. Michelle Pfeiffer plays a single mother of a little boy whose schoolmate is George Clooney's daughter. When their kids miss a scheduled field trip, the two adults frantically try to balance the demands of work, parenthood, and potential romance. The premise was sparked by producer Lynda Obst's own over-committed schedule. "I was having a spectacularly impossible day, logistically, in which I was trying to do my job and deal with the exigencies of a teenage son. My situation, it turned out, was quite similar to that of several of my friends who had their own share of hellacious career/child-juggling days. I suddenly realized that the new definition of heroism was simply surviving the day as a working mother." *One Fine Day* screenwriter Ellen Simon knew how to turn this noodle of an idea into a full-blown story, "I'm always drawn to real situations stretched to the point where they become funny, and focused to the place where they become true."

Real situations stretched to the point they become funny, and focused to the place where they become true—what a wonderful explanation of how wishful thinking becomes chick flick reality.

CHAPTER 3

Improving Perfection

Remakes, Sequels, and Other Movie Makeovers

W hile some movie plotlines hatch full blown from a screenwriter's active imagination, many of the best are based on previously existing material. Biographies, plays, and novels make wonderful source material—as do chick flicks themselves. The thinking goes, if a movie worked once, there's no reason why it can't work again—either as a sequel, or perhaps remade, updated, Americanized, or even turned into a musical. Luckily for us, there are excellent veins of potential chick flick source material out there, just waiting to be mined.

Literary Adaptations

CASE STUDY: EMMA (1996)

As fans of Bobbie Ann Mason's *In Country* well know, there's nothing worse than a beloved novel being turned into a not-so-wonderful movie.

But when the adaptation works, when the movie version is just as good as the book or even better, chick flick enthusiasts jump for joy.

While every major Jane Austen novel has been filmed at least once, *Emma* has proven particularly popular. Available for rent at your local video store are a 1972 BBC version (lesser known, but still available on home video), a 1996 American film with chick flick superstar Gwyneth Paltrow in the title role, and a 1997 A&E television production staring Kate Beckinsale (helpfully identified on video boxes as *Jane Austen's Emma*).

Why does an 1816 novel about an inept matchmaker causing havoc among the denizens of a small English village remain such a wellspring? "There's a dearth of good modern material, so I think people come to her work with renewed delight," theorizes 1996's *Emma* writer/director Douglas McGrath. "It's so well thought out, in terms of character and story—and there's always the gratifying thrill that self-recognition brings!" Additionally, the cinematic depiction of nineteenth-century lifestyle is scrumptious: the clothes, the mansions, the formal dances, the countryside, it's a romance novel come to life.

Literary Adaptations Modernized, Americanized, and Set in High School

CASE STUDY: CLUELESS (1995)

Emma has such resiliency as movie fodder that it has also been Americanized as a teen flick. With 1995's *Clueless*, writer/director Amy Heckerling drags Jane Austen's heroine into the late twentieth century and plops her down in Beverly Hills, California. Emma's now named Cher, but she still has a self-involved but loving father and a hunky older not-quite-brother love interest. Her makeover project is an uncouth trans-fer student (played by not-yet-hot-in-real-life Brittany Murphy). So many of the plot's details translate nicely to the modern age (i.e., instead of sketching her protégé, Cher photographs her for the yearbook) that this adaptation proves that Jane Austen remains the undefeated queen bee of Chick Flicks.

Shakespeare also does well modernized, Americanized, and "teenagized." Julia Stiles has starred in two kick-ass reinterpretations: 1999's *10 Things I Hate About You* (*Taming of the Shrew*) and 2001's *O* (*Othello*).

Old Movies Remade and Updated

CASE STUDY: SABRINA (1954)
AND SABRINA (1995)

Who would dare remake an Audrey Hepburn chick flick classic? Direc-tor Sydney Pollack. "The question I asked myself going into the project was, 'Can you mix the economic attitudes of the Nineties with the ro-mantic fairy tale of the Fifties?,' " explains Pollack, who updated the story of Sabrina, a chauffeur's daughter who thinks she's in love with playboy David but ultimately falls for his staid businessman brother, Li-nus. "I was lucky enough to get [original director] Billy Wilder to talk about ways to contemporize the script. I stole as many of the highlights of the old movie as I could. But I felt that this version could be much more an examination of Linus [Harrison Ford's character] as a charac-ter, and that intrigued me."

Okay, so maybe the story could be updated, but who would dare to improve on Audrey Hepburn?! "Julia Ormond has a combination of intelligence and gravity that makes her quite original and distinctive," rationalizes Pollack. "She's not quite like anyone else. There's no attempt to walk in Audrey Hepburn's shoes at all because we are coming at this from an entirely different direction." When the remake first surfaced in 1995, many devotees refused to be won over, but during the ensuing years a sizable fan base has grown for the newer version.

Foreign Movies Remade and Americanized

CASE STUDY: WINGS OF DESIRE (1988) AND CITY OF ANGELS (1998)

American directors have mined some of the great foreign films for remake material. *City of Angels* is based on the well-regarded Wim Wenders's film, *Wings of Desire*. In the German original, Bruno Ganz is a melancholic angel haunting a black-and-white Berlin. The American version identifies Los Angeles as the city of angels, throws in color, includes a cool Goo Goo Dolls song on the soundtrack, recasts Nicolas Cage as the angel, and adds a new romantic subplot involving Meg Ryan as a heartsick heart surgeon.

So did original director Wim Wenders think his story got better with Meg Ryan involved? "I knew that [American director] Brad Silberling had a great script to begin with," Wenders cautiously admits. "[Hollywood screenwriter] Dana Stevens had translated my Berlin story into a real L.A. story with a lot of feeling. And I knew that Brad had a marvelous cast with Nicolas Cage and Meg Ryan. Still, when I sat down in that theater and watched the film for the first time, I was really nervous. To watch a remake of your own film, that must be quite a rare occasion. Anyway, it had never happened to me before. It felt like being a grandfather or something. I am not responsible for anything up there on the screen, and yet I was, in a strange way. It could have turned into a painful experience, but it didn't. Not at all. On the contrary, I liked what I saw a lot. It was moving, it was beautifully crafted, there was some amazing imagry and an astonishing story. I had never seen anything like it. Well, except for that one German film maybe, with the subtitles . . . what was its name again?"

Old Movies Turned into Musicals

CASE STUDY: THE PHILADELPHIA STORY (1940) AND HIGH SOCIETY (1956)

Messing around with the soundtrack is an audacious way to give an old story a new spin. Originally based on a hit play, *The Philadelphia Story* first hit the big screen with Katherine Hepburn portraying a judgmental socialite whose wedding plans go awry when her ex-husband (Cary Grant) and a tabloid reporter (Jimmy Stewart) invade her household. When it was remade a decade and a half later with Grace Kelly in Hepburn's shoes, crooner Bing Crosby as the ex, and singing sensation Frank

Sinatra as the reporter, tunes like "True Love" and "Now You Has Jazz" were added. The resulting musical is just as delightful as the original, and has the added benefit of an all-star soundtrack.

Sequels

CASE STUDY: DIRTY DANCING (1987) AND DIRTY DANCING: HAVANA NIGHTS (2004)

Let's not forget about sequels. If the first movie struck a chord with viewers, why not supply the demand for more? The problem is that successful chick flicks by definition conclude with a satisfying ending: the leads either live happily ever after or they don't, and there's nothing more to say. Nevertheless, sequel makers know fans of the original film want a second serving, preferably something more than reheated leftovers.

In *Dirty Dancing: Havana Nights*, rather than continue the romance between Jennifer Grey's character, Baby, and her dance partner, Patrick Swayze's Johnny, the story is reset in 1958 Cuba, where a brand new sexy couple (Diego Luna and Romola Garai) indulge in a slightly different style of scandalous dancing. It's a terrific way of giving fans of the original the same story with a new flavor.

An even better sequel idea comes from France: the 1986 film *A Man and A Woman: 20 Years Later*. The impossibly stylish 1966 original starred Jean-Louis Trintignant and Anouk Aimée as a race car driver and a widow who fall in love. The sequel, as the title promises, catches up with them two decades later, both actors having aged very gracefully. What a fabulous idea—to reunite treasured chick flick lovers long after fans have given up hope that a sequel would ever materialize. Hollywood, take note! Can't wait for the year 2010, and the possibility of *Pretty Woman: 20 Years Later*.

CHAPTER 4

Preaching to the Choir

You Are Destined to Find Your True Love and Other Timeless Themes

W hile sometimes a shopping montage is simply a shopping montage, the various elements contained in a chick flick should add up to a coherent whole. Before the curtain falls, the audience is presented with a message-filled scenario that we can either accept or reject as we see fit. "The common bond that everybody can relate to is love," proclaims *Boys on the Side* star Drew Barrymore, who further enthuses, "I love 'love.'" Who doesn't love love? But do chick flicks like *Boys on the Side* offer a message any more substantial than love is lovely? While there are indeed more momentous messages being sent out into the world under such innocuous titles as *You've Got Mail*, most of the optimistic and empowering life lessons contained in chick flicks are almost Oprah-worthy. Let's give the creators (the writers, directors, producers, and stars) a chance to explain their films' deeper meanings in their own words.

Life Lesson: Life Is about the Journey, Not the Destination.

CASE STUDY: BOYS ON THE SIDE (1995)

In *Boys on the Side*, an odd troika of women—Whoopi Goldberg as a lesbian songbird, Mary-Louise Parker as an AIDS patient, and Drew Barrymore as a pregnant murderess—embark on a road trip fraught with misadventures. While promoting the film, the late director Herbert Ross pointed out, "The road in this film is really a conduit through which these women find each other and through which they discover that life is not necessarily about where you are going, but how you get there."

Life Lesson: Always Listen to Your Heart.

CASE STUDY: FOUR WEDDINGS AND A FUNERAL (1994)

In *Four Weddings and a Funeral*, Hugh Grant and Andie MacDowell are immediately attracted to each other when they meet at the first of the four weddings. Yet she marries another man in wedding number three. Putting major thought into what motivates her character's bad decision, Andie MacDowell concluded that "Carrie is a very modern woman, but I don't think she's ever been in love. She's a woman who uses her brains rather than her heart. Carrie's experienced a lot in life, she's very independent, and very self-assured. She meets Hamish [the wrong husband], who is extremely kind and loves her and she feels safe with him. She believes she loves him without listening to her heartbeat—which is Charles [Hugh Grant's character]." Not to ruin the ending for anyone who hasn't seen it yet, but Andie finally wises up after Hugh almost marries some-one else. The movie ends with the two lovebirds standing in the rain, promising not to get married to anyone else.

Life Lesson: Change is Possible.
You Can Improve Your Life by Ridding Yourself of Self-Imposed Constraints.

CASE STUDY: CHOCOLAT (2000)

In *Chocolat*, Juliette Binoche plays Vianne, a woman who comes from a family of itinerant chocolate makers. She and her young daughter arrive in a small French town to open a sweets shop, but hostile reaction from the town bigwig encourages her to move on. "Vianne is a wanderer, and she expects to always keep moving. But I don't think she necessarily wants this life," Mademoiselle Binoche confides. "It's a pattern inside her and she can't yet pull herself away from it. She has an enormous struggle inside her that many people face: between the way her life was as a child, and the way she wants to live now. It's something we all struggle with— to break from our parents and our past and live our own lives." In the movie, Juliette's young daughter protests her mother's decision to leave. Thanks to the friendship of the town women and the support of love in-terest Johnny Depp, Juliette and her daughter decide to stay and plant roots.

Life Lesson: There Is Rhyme and Reason to the Universe. It's Called Destiny.

CASE STUDY: SERENDIPITY (2001)

In the John Cusack/Kate Beckinsale romance *Serendipity*, John and Kate meet by chance buying a pair of gloves at Bloomingdales. Attracted to each other, but both committed to others, the two would-be lovers inscribe their names and phone numbers on a book and a five-dollar bill. The theory is that if they later come across those random objects, then they are fated to be together. Days away from marrying, John makes a last-ditch effort to reconnect with Kate. After a series of near-misses, the two finally find each other. "It clearly affirms that there is a grand master plan to things," states star Cusack. "And if that is true, then that is a very comforting notion."

Life Lesson: Ordinary People Can Lead Extraordinary Lives.

CASE STUDY: WHILE YOU WERE SLEEPING (1995)

You can't get much more ordinary than Sandra Bullock's Chicago subway worker heroine in *While You Were Sleeping*. Secretly in love with a man she sees every day on the platform, Sandra is mistaken for the man's fiancée when she rescues him during a coma-inducing accident. "[The former Columbia studio head] Dawn Steel [once] said to me that one of the things she loves to see in films is ordinary people doing extraordinary things," reveals the film's director, Jon Turteltaub. "In this story, you have Lucy [Sandra Bullock's character] who is theoretically an ordinary person going through an extraordinary time, pushing herself to new limits and being overwhelmed. Instead of doing it just for the sake of falling in love with a man, she does it for the sake of finding out what is missing in that empty spot." Ultimately, she decides to stop hiding from life in her dead-end job and pursue some of her dreams.

Life Lesson: You Can Make It Through Anything.

CASE STUDY: HOPE FLOATS (1998)

What would you do if you went on a daytime talk show with your best friend who then reveals on national television that she's sleeping with your husband? Sandra Bullock decides to move back to her mother's house. Unfortunately, many people in her hometown seem to delight in the downfall of the former beauty queen. Sandra Bullock not only starred in *Hope Floats*, she produced it. "I felt that *Hope Floats* was a special story which tells us that although life may be really difficult at times, there can be a light at the end of the tunnel to which we can aim." Another one of the film's producers agrees, "It's about starting over again and what happens when the perfect picture you thought defined your life crumbles before your eyes. In the end, we learn that even the most emotionally troubling events can help us find our destiny."

Life Lesson: You Will Find Your True Prince.
CASE STUDY: WHAT A GIRL WANTS (2003)

Raised by a bohemian single mother, American teenager Amanda Bynes never knew her British aristocrat father Colin Firth. Needing to connect with her MIA pop, Amanda hightails it across the Atlantic to introduce herself. Surprised but delighted, Colin takes the uncouth teen into his snooty household. Can a *My Fair Lady* transformation be far behind? "I think every young girl dreams of finding her prince," points out producer Denise DiNovi, who reports that *What a Girl Wants* was inspired by a 1958 Sandra Dee-Rex Harrison romantic comedy called *The Reluctant Debutante*. "In *What a Girl Wants*, we have a girl who longs to make her fairy tale fantasy come true, but the prince she is searching for is her father."

Life Lesson: Celebrate What Is Special about Your Life.
CASE STUDY: RUNAWAY BRIDE (1999)

In the long-awaited re-pairing of Julia Roberts and Richard Gere, Julia is the title character, a woman with a bad habit of leaving grooms at the altar, and Richard is the cynical newspaper reporter who's come to town to write her story. "Maggie [Julia's character] has run away from marriage several times—there's a reason for that," explains director Garry Marshall. "She has been a chameleon in her relationships, transforming herself into the person she thinks her boyfriend wants her to be. It's only where she becomes true to herself that she has a shot at true happiness." Roberts agrees, "At the beginning of the film, with all her cheeky qualities, Maggie doesn't really have a voice for herself. And that is what she comes to find by the end of the movie—an ability to say what she feels when she is feeling it, as opposed to censoring things or worrying about extraneous things that don't have anything to do with her or her relationships." Garry Marshall hastens to add, "I hope audiences will come away with the feeling that you don't have to put on an act to find love, but to be true to yourself. Everybody deserves to be loved for the unique person they are."

Life Lesson: Be Yourself and You Will Succeed.

CASE STUDY: LEGALLY BLONDE (2001)

Can a bubble-headed California blonde be a spokesperson for girl power? She can if she's Reese Witherspoon's Elle Woods, a sorority sister who leaves superficiality behind to join her boyfriend at law school. Sure, her bikini-clad admission video secured her a spot at the institute of higher learning, but she has doubts whether her own brand of street smarts will triumph in the courtroom. Reese explains, "Everybody has a moment in their lives where they stop believing in themselves. But Elle proves with her own special spirit that anyone can overcome their fears and succeed on their own terms, whatever those might be. Some people might succeed because they know Plato and Socrates, and other people succeed because they know about Porsches and Clinique. The point is to use what you have and to believe in yourselves."

Amen, sister.

CHAPTER 5

America's Sweethearts
The Quintessential Female Superstars

I t's not easy being a chick flick superstar. Often the top divas who define the genre want to stretch their acting chops and move beyond their defined boundaries. Sometimes their audiences will go with them on these side trips, but mostly we want them playing the same kind of characters we know and love.

What makes an actress a superstar? Being mega-love-worthy is the number one requirement for becoming America's Sweetheart. "I love Drew," swears Barrymore's *The Wedding Singer* co-star, Adam Sandler. "Everyone loves Drew," Sandler clarifies. "My mother loves her, and even the birds in my backyard love her." Despite being mega-love-worthy, it's hard for these actresses to find appropriate male co-stars to play Romeo to their on-screen Juliets. What's worse, many of these women suffer this problem in their real lives as well. Their personal stories are proof that real life can be just like a chick flick, especially for chick flick superstars.

The Ultimate Superstar: Julia Roberts

Mike Newell, who directed Julia Roberts in *Mona Lisa Smile*, reports Roberts "has an innate connection to audiences. They feel, very strongly, that they know her, and they like her." *Mona Lisa Smile* co-star Maggie Gyllenhaal admits, "I was fascinated by her, the way she moved, the way she walked, the way she connected with people. She's a focused, clear, strong woman, which is key to her appeal around the world. At the same time, there's a vulnerability. She can get so emotional you think she could crack at any moment. That's why her characters seem like real people, women who are strong, complicated, overwhelming and sometimes overwhelmed."

Amazingly, almost from her first moment on screen, Julia Roberts was ordained a superstar. Thanks to 1988's *Mystic Pizza*, 1989's *Steel Magnolias*, and 1990's *Pretty Woman*, she became an unstoppable megastar.

Not only is Julia the number one female box office champ worldwide, her personal love life is pure chick flick material. For many years, J.Ro (as George Clooney jokingly calls her) suffered from extreme Bad Boyfriend Syndrome, hooking up with a series of moody male actors (Kiefer Sutherland, Jason Patric, Benjamin Bratt). When she did find someone she thought might be her destiny, he seemed like a genuine hero: a witty singer/songwriter from Texas. However, anyone who saw Julia and Lyle Lovett's wedding photo on the July 12, 1993, cover of *People* knew the marriage wouldn't last—our chick flick goddess looked god-awful in her bridal gown. On the surface, her second marriage to cameraman Danny Moder seems much more mundane, but again it's prime chick flick material: the world's biggest female movie star fell in love with a regular guy. Very *Notting Hill*.

Under-Appreciated Gems Double Feature:

Rediscover the glory of Julia Roberts with this offbeat double feature showcasing two of her under-appreciated gems:

- *Mystic Pizza* (1988)—Julia plays a hot-tempered Portuguese waitress who falls for a rich hotshot, much to the dismay of her hardworking mother, sister, and best friend. Look for a very young Matt Damon in a quick cameo as the boyfriend's brother. Tip for the hardcore J.Ro fan: If you covet the "A Slice of Heaven" T-shirt Julia wears in the flick, you can order your own from the real Mystic Pizza in Mystic, Connecticut.

- *Sleeping with the Enemy* (1991)—Ms. Roberts no longer does these "wife fights back against her evil husband" roles, leaving them to Ashley Judd and Jennifer Lopez. In this early flick, she fakes her own death to escape the abusive Patrick Bergin.

First Runner-up: Meg Ryan

Meg Ryan likes bad boys. She married Dennis Quaid when he was a wild one, helped tame him, and produced an impossibly cute son, whom they both adore. When filming *Proof of Life* with Russell Crowe, she fell for the Australian bad boy. Divorcing Dennis, Meg happily cavorted with the smoldering Crowe. That red-hot affair soon cooled, leaving Ms. Ryan a glamorous single mother in search of her true Prince Charming. Meg Ryan is just so mega-love-worthy and cute (and has such great hair) that we all know one day her prince will come.

As a chick flick superstar, Meg Ryan has already found her prince: Tom Hanks. "I think Tom and Meg share something, which is that men and women love them in equal amounts," postulates *Sleepless in Seattle* and *You've Got Mail* writer/director Nora Ephron. Ephron has an additional theory: "You know how often you see married couples who almost look as if they've cast each other? They kind of look as if they belong together. Tom and Meg look as if they belong together. That's the truth." Of course, in real life, Tom Hanks is happily married to someone else.

Under-Appreciated Gems Double Feature:

- *When a Man Loves a Woman* (1994)—A darker Meg Ryan piece. She's an alcoholic slipping out of control, and Andy Garcia is the husband who wants to save her.

- *I.Q.* (1994)—In this quirky romantic comedy, Ms. Ryan plays the niece of Albert Einstein. Determined to marry a genius like her uncle, she wrongly discounts garage monkey Tim Robbins in favor of stuffy Stephen Fry.

Second Runner-Up: Sandra Bullock

Poor Sandra Bullock. With no Oscars on her shelf and no Tracy and Hepburn–like reteaming with her perfect on-screen match, Sandra trails behind Julia and Meg in the chick flick superstar pageant. But don't underestimate her. "People might look at what she does and think it's easy," points out Bullock's *Two Weeks Notice* director Marc Lawrence, "but in fact it's incredibly difficult. She makes a scene funny *and* real. She's a gifted physical comedienne with great comic instincts and remarkable truth-telling in her work."

As for Bullock's personal life, as long as she remains "friends" with Matthew McConaughey, how is she going to find true love? Sandra's been involved with several of her co-stars (including *Love Potion #9*'s Tate Donovan and the much younger Ryan Gossling from her 2002 cop flick, *Murder by Numbers*), but the one guy whom she seems to always go back to is Matthew McConaughey. They even vacation together—as friends.

Chick flick enthusiasts know where this relationship is heading. Or maybe not. Matthew McConaughey is one of those tricky guys who are so hard to nail down—is he a best friend, bad boy, bad boyfriend, or true prince? He was once arrested for playing bongos in the nude, so what does that say about him? Perhaps Sandra still hasn't figured it out. Looks like Ms. Bullock's life is ready for a plot twist.

Under-Appreciated Gems Double Feature:

- *The Thing Called Love* (1993)—Sandra's a supporting actress in this Nashville-set story, which was co-star River Phoenix's last completed film. Playing an aspiring country music singer named Linda Lue Linden, our Sandy sings a ditty she composed herself.

- *Forces of Nature* (1999)—Bullock plays a kook who drives straight-laced Ben Affleck wild in this road trip/screwball comedy. Affleck proved to be the bad boyfriend character in real life for Gwyneth Paltrow and Jennifer Lopez. Maybe he's Sandra Bullock's true prince. Watch the film closely for clues that he might secretly find her love-worthy.

Third Runner-Up: Jennifer Lopez

Jennifer Lopez is a triple threat: a dancer-singer-actress who started her career as one of the background dancers on the TV series *In Living Color*. Ms. Lopez, a.k.a. J.Lo, is also a tabloid queen, with a love life that remains constant headline fodder. Married young, Jen remains friendly with her first ex, whom she later hired to run a restaurant she owns (add another career to her resume—also add clothing designer and perfume maven while you're at it). Next, Ms. Lopez was famously involved with the rap impresario Sean "Puffy" Combs. After breaking up with Puffy, J.Lo tried to play it safe by marrying one of her background dancers. Yes, the background dancer who clawed her way up to the top married a lowly background dancer. Very *A Star Is Born*. Of course, that marriage didn't last. The second ex went on a reality television show called *I'm a Celebrity, Get Me Out of Here!* Although it's questionable how much of a celebrity Cris Judd is without being identified as Mr. Jennifer Lopez, he did win the contest and proved himself to be a really nice guy.

For a short time, when making *The Wedding Planner*, J.Lo was unattached. "When I signed on to the film, my life really mirrored [my character] Mary's," Ms. Lopez fondly remembers. "I was very focused on my career, and I put my love life on the back burner at that time." Her love life was back in the magazine headlines when she began a high profile romance with Ben Affleck. Their scheduled wedding was derailed by the overwhelming media attention. She bounced back with a quickie marriage to singer Marc Anthony. While we can all hope the third time's a charm for Jenny from the Block, perhaps Ms. Lopez and Cris Judd should watch *The Philadelphia Story* or *High Society*; he might be the ex-husband she should re-wed.

Under-Appreciated Gems Double Feature:

- *Enough* (2002)—Like fellow tough chicks Ashley Judd and Angelina Jolie, Jennifer Lopez excels at action/thrillers. In this one, she plays a poor waitress who has to fight evil husband Billy Campbell to save her young daughter.

- *Selena* (1997)—In this star-making bioflick, Jen sings and dances up a storm as she portrays the doomed pop star. Unfortunately, the real life Selena wore stage costumes that would make anyone's butt look huge, let alone Ms. Lopez's, who is deservedly famous for her curvaceous posterior.

Fourth Runner-Up: Drew Barrymore

The youngest in a long line of acting Barrymores, Drew fancies herself a free sprit. She has dated rock stars and eagerly posed nude for famous photographers. Her impulsive first marriage (to a bartender) was very short lived. She next married gross-out MTV comedian Tom Green, and then quickly divorced him. With two marriages under her belt before her thirtieth birthday, Drew is once again dating musicians. When will this wild child grasp the basic chick flick tenet that free spirits find real romance when they devote their energies to loosening up uptight love-worthy heroes?

Under-Appreciated Gems Double Feature:

- *Riding in Cars with Boys* (2001)—Barrymore plays a teenage mother determined to better herself. Watch Drew age two decades as the movie tracks her relationship with her son.

- *Mad Love* (1995)—Drew's "crazy chick"/road trip flick. Chris O'Donnell is the straightlaced love interest here, more convincing as Drew's sidekick than he was as Batman's Robin.

Honorable Mention: Gwyneth Paltrow

Coming from a show biz family (mother is an actress, late beloved father was a television and film director), Gwyneth Paltrow has been around the business her whole life. She dated Brad Pitt for years, basically training him to be a good red carpet husband for Jennifer Aniston. When she was with Brad, they often had matching hair color. Gwen then dated Ben Affleck, who resisted the matching tresses but was willing to face the paparazzi with her. It was good training for him when he subsequently hooked up with flashbulb queen Jennifer Lopez. An American who excels at portraying Englishwomen on the big screen, Gwen now resides in London with her very own Englishman, Chris Martin, the lead singer from the rock group Coldplay. The new Mr. Gwyneth Paltrow isn't as media friendly as her past beaux, lashing out at photographers and whatnot, but he'll soon learn how to play the fame game.

Under-Appreciated Gems Double Feature:

- *Sliding Doors* (1998)—In this Brit piece, Gwyneth catches her man with another woman, then sees what her life would have been like if that event had never taken place.

- *Bounce* (2000)—Gwen's a young widow who doesn't know that handsome Ben Affleck is paying her attention because he inadvertently caused her husband's death. Affleck looked uncomfortable when he played screen lover to his then real-life lover Jennifer Lopez in *Gigli*, but he's terrific romancing Gwen in this drama. Look for *Dirty Dancing*'s Jennifer Grey (post-nosejob) as Ben's pal.

Most Promising Newcomer: Reese Witherspoon

Reese Witherspoon started out as a child star, although not as famous as Drew Barrymore. Like Drew, she has matured into a very sunny, mega-love-worthy young lady. A Southerner like Julia, perky and blonde like Meg, funny like Sandra, and comfortable in British period pieces like Gwyneth, Reese seems to be an unbeatable amalgamation of those who have come before her. And like several of her predecessors, she's found love with a co-star, Ryan Phillippe from *Cruel Intentions*. However, Reese must watch out: her husband's occasional flippant comments about his wife's superstardom status and the resulting inequality of their careers indicates that there might be a few bumps in the road ahead.

Under-Appreciated Gems Double Feature:

- *The Man in the Moon* (1991)—Preteen Reese has a crush on a neighbor boy who loves her older sister. (Fair warning: It's a tearjerker.)

- *Overnight Delivery* (1996)—Paul Rudd is desperate to stop a break-up letter from being delivered. A brunette Reese plays a stripper tagging along for the ride.

The Quintessential Chick Flick
Superstar of All Time: Audrey Hepburn

From Mary Pickford to Molly Ringwald, from Doris Day to Alicia Silverstone, each generation of moviegoers has embraced certain actresses as America's Sweetheart. However the reigning champ who continues to appeal to each new generation is everyone's fair lady, Audrey Hepburn. Like today's superstars, Ms. Hepburn seems to have lived a chick flick life. After surviving a horrible childhood in war-torn Europe, she got her big break playing Gigi on stage. With her gamine looks, it was only a matter of time before she became a movie star. She married a fellow actor, Mel Ferrer, and had a child with him, but the marriage didn't last. She married once again (to a nonactor), had another son, and another divorce. Late in life, she fell in love with a much younger nonactor and found happiness. In addition to her acting career and her sons, she found fulfillment as a hands-on spokeswoman for UNICEF before her tearjerker ending, tragically succumbing to the ravages of cancer at the age of sixty-four.

Under-Appreciated Gems Double Feature:

- *How to Steal a Million* (1966)—Ms. Hepburn pairs up with an impossibly young and handsome Peter O'Toole in this caper set in Paris, in which the dynamic duo attempt to liberate a questionably valuable statue from a well-guarded art museum.

- *Two for the Road* (1967)—In this complicated portrait of a marriage, Ms. Hepburn travels the French countryside with another impossibly handsome young Brit, Albert Finney. Hollywood production companies keep threatening to remake this flick, but who could top the remarkably stylish original?

CHAPTER 6

Hunks Wanted

Prince Charming Personified

A s hard as it is for a quintessential chick flick superstar to find a suitable mate in real life, it's even harder for her to score the perfect on-screen love interest. "To find just the right chemistry with someone isn't easy," sighs Sandra Bullock. Not only must the leading man have acting chops equal to one of the biggest female stars in the world, he has to embody a hero that the audience will endorse as worthy of our heroine's affection—or the romance won't jell. To raise the stakes further, the actor must rely on his own personal charisma to make an often-unlikable or one-dimensional character love-worthy. In short, the obligatory hunk has to have sex appeal. Explaining why Aidan Quinn, for example, worked so well as Sandra Bullock's love interest in *Practical Magic*, producer Denise DiNovi recalls, "We chose Aidan because he has a very poetic feeling about him, but he is also very grounded, warm, and manly." Screenwriter Josann McGibbon is more candid about why she went nuts over a then-unknown Brad Pitt's audition for her romantic comedy, *The Favor*: "He was adorable. I desperately wanted to be ten years younger."

Director Sofia Coppola also remembers evaluating each actor's sex appeal quotient when casting the hunk role for *The Virgin Suicides*. "Trip had to be an incredible, out-of-this-world dreamy cute guy," proclaims Sofia. "We interviewed a lot of cute actors, but I wanted somebody with a real presence, somebody who had that swagger that gets you the moment you see him on the street, like a young Matt Dillon." She ended up casting Josh Hartnett, now a major teen heartthrob. "Not only was he incredibly handsome, but he was a really great actor. He was very exciting to watch."

If all it took were massive amounts of pheromones, George Clooney would star in every chick flick made today. A more decisive factor, especially when dealing with the superstar hunks, is their willingness to forgo a big paycheck headlining a macho action flick to sign on as Kate Hudson's boyfriend—for a lot less money. With rare exception, George Clooney would rather invite Julia Roberts to take a supporting role in his *Ocean's Eleven* franchise than make another *One Fine Day* with Michelle Pfeiffer. On the other hand, because wooing Michelle Pfeiffer can be a lot more fun than saving the world from computer-generated aliens, an action star is sometimes willing to trade in his combat gear for a wedding suit. "When [director] Lewis Gilbert asked me to do *Educating Rita*," recalls Michael Caine, "I was delighted, because I've done those special effects films, you know, staring at a 'blue screen' for six weeks with the lasers or whatever added to the film much later on, or getting soaked by ninety-three tons of water. I've done all that."

Mel Gibson also feels the need to justify his decision to do a fluffy chick flick like *What Women Want* instead of another manly epic adventure like *Braveheart*. "The story has to be compelling, whether it's a battle picture or a living room weeper, it doesn't matter so long as there is truth to it," Gibson rationalizes. "That said, I think it's more difficult to do a romantic comedy. You can't be false or too over the top because it's immediately, obviously not funny. As Nancy [Meyers, the director] often quotes, 'Dying is easy, comedy is hard.' And if you're not funny, believe me, you die up there."

His *What Women Want* co-star Helen Hunt says Mel passed the test. "All you have to be is smart and willing in a romantic comedy, and Mel so completely embodies those qualities. He is incredibly sharp, has a great sense of humor, and is willing to take risks. You have to be ready to look silly, to go almost too far, but you also need the brains to keep it grounded in reality so that people care while they're laughing."

Poetic, grounded, warm, manly, adorable, out-of-this-world dreamy cute, has a real presence, has that swagger that gets you the moment you see him, incredibly handsome, very exciting to watch, incredibly sharp, has a great sense of humor, and is willing to take risks—sounds like a personal ad, doesn't it? If such a "hunk wanted" notice ran, any one of the following gentlemen would definitely get a call.

The Ultimate Chick Flick Prince Charming: Hugh Grant

Hugh Grant learned firsthand that it's not so easy to duplicate chick flick hero behavior in real life. One summer night in 1995, he apparently decided he was ready to be Richard Gere and pick up his own pretty woman off the streets of Hollywood. Whereas Richard's character found true love and happiness, Hugh found himself busted by the cops. Unlike many celebrities who look like hell in their mug shot, Hugh looked just like a Hugh Grant character would look—sheepish, yet charming. The public forgave him for his indiscretion, and his longtime girlfriend Elizabeth Hurley stood by him. After a decent period of time, Hugh and Liz called it quits, and she got involved with a millionaire playboy who impregnated her and then fiercely denied paternity. If their romance were in a chick flick, Hugh and Liz would ultimately end up together. At this point, they're both still single.

Prince Charming Double Feature:

- *Bridget Jones's Diary* (2001)—Granted, in this Renée Zellweger/ Hugh Grant/Colin Firth romantic triangle, Hugh plays the bad boyfriend. But come on, take a look at him emerging soaking wet from a dunking in the lake—just as sexy as Colin Firth's dip in *Pride and Prejudice*.

- *Love Actually* (2003)—Another Hugh Grant vehicle written by *Four Weddings and a Funeral* scribe Richard Curtis. This time Hugh's the Prime Minister—yet still sexy, and still desperate for a date. Colin Firth is also in this ensemble piece (playing a writer in love with a woman who doesn't speak English).

First Runner-Up: Colin Firth

While he has played his share of bad boyfriends (*Shakespeare in Love* and *The English Patient* are particular standouts), Colin Firth's signature Prince Charming role is Mr. Darcy in the 300-minute BBC/A&E adaptation of Jane Austen's *Pride and Prejudice*. Firth, typical male, hadn't read the book and didn't understand the power of his role. "But then when I mentioned it," he marvels, "everyone would tell me how they were devoted to this book, how at school they'd been in love with Darcy, and my brother said, 'Darcy? Isn't he supposed to be sexy?'"

Poor Colin is now forever associated with his character. In fact, he's been forced to play Darcy again and again in *Bridget Jones's Diary* (a *Clueless*-like very loose adaptation/modernization of *Pride and Prejudice*) and its sequel, *Bridget Jones: The Edge of Reason*. Luckily, Colin likes the Darcy character in all its incarnations, claiming, "I think he's actually extremely emotional and passionate. He has all the qualities that make a person dynamic yet they're all closed in this very formal English straight jacket." True to form, Colin had not read the *Bridget Jones's Diary* book before agreeing to do the part. Someone, get Colin Firth a library card!

Prince Charming Double Feature:

- *Pride and Prejudice* (1995)—Buy the DVD so you can enjoy all five hours of Elizabeth's romance with Darcy whenever you want.

- *The Importance of Being Earnest* (2002)—In this Oscar Wilde comedy, Colin and *My Best Friend's Wedding*'s Rupert Everett both serenade Reese Witherspoon.

Second Runner-Up: George Clooney

Former co-stars Nicole Kidman (*The Peacemaker*) and Michelle Pfeiffer (*One Fine Day*) both bet perpetual bachelor George Clooney $10,000 that he'd be married with children by the time he turned forty. That birthday came and went, and there's still no current Mrs. Clooney. Having married and divorced actress Talia Balsam early in his career, George is having too much fun as a carefree Romeo to tie himself down again. Having established his reputation as a heartthrob on the television medical series *ER* and been named Sexiest Man Alive by *People* in 1997, George resists playing his assigned role of Prince Charming on the big screen. Instead of giving us full-on chick flicks, he'd rather do quirky art house films like *Solaris*, macho action adventures like *The Perfect Storm* or Coen Brothers cartoonish comedies like *Intolerable Cruelty*. We can only hope he'll settle down one fine day.

Prince Charming Double Feature:

- *One Fine Day* (1996)—Director Michael Hoffman cites *Pat and Mike*, *The Philadelphia Story*, *Adam's Rib*, and *It Happened One Night* as antecedents to this battle-of-the-sexes romance between single mother Michelle Pfeiffer and divorced dad George Clooney. Made while he was still playing Dr. Ross on TV, this is Clooney's only flat-out chick flick to date. George himself says this romance has "a kind of *Pillow Talk* vibe."

- *Out of Sight* (1998)—This Elmore Leonard crime caper (made by many of the same people responsible for *Get Shorty*) benefits from very sexy performances from gorgeous George as an unrepentant bank robber and Jennifer Lopez as the law enforcement agent who finds him irresistible.

Third Runner-Up: Brad Pitt

Like pretty actresses who downplay their looks for serious roles, Brad Pitt is always fighting against his stunning beauty. Like his predecessor Robert Redford, Brad would prefer that we look beyond his golden exterior and appreciate his darker interior. While Redford occasionally submits to pressure and delivers sparkling chick flicks like *Barefoot in the Park*, *The Way We Were*, and *Up Close and Personal*, Brad isn't as gracious. For example, he makes a road trip picture with Julia Roberts, and instead of the chick flick delight it should be, *The Mexican* turns out to be a grungy action piece.

Fortunately, Pitt makes up for his lackluster cinematic output by being an extra-fabulous love interest in real life. When Brad was with Gwyneth Paltrow, he looked impossibly handsome accompanying her to premieres and has said nothing but nice things about her since they broke up. And when Brad married Jennifer Aniston, it was clear from the single publicity photo they released to the press that he was marrying his true love.

Prince Charming Double Feature:

- *Interview with the Vampire—The Vampire Chronicles* (1994)— Who would have ever thought Anne Rice's novel would get made with Brad, Tom Cruise, Antonio Banderas, and a very young Kirsten Dunst as the sexy vampires?

- *Ocean's Eleven* (2001)—In this flashy caper set in Vegas, Brad Pitt is George Clooney's partner in crime. A remake of an old Rat Pack flick, Julia Roberts also appears, taking on the old Angie Dickinson role as Clooney's main squeeze.

Fourth Runner-Up: Nicolas Cage

I've seen Nicolas Cage in person several times, and I can attest that he always radiates sexuality. If you didn't know he was a movie star, you'd think he should be one. In fact, Nic comes from a show business family (*Lost in Translation* director Sofia Coppola and *Rushmore* star Jason Schwartzman are his first cousins). He changed his last name from Coppola to Cage to avoid accusations of nepotism, yet he couldn't resist the strong pull of family ties and took early acting gigs in his uncle Francis Ford Coppola's films (a small bit in *Rumble Fish*, and a very large role as a nerd in *Peggy Sue Got Married*). After putting his animal magnetism to good use in *Moonstruck* (no one objected that he was too young for Cher!), Nicolas Cage squandered his talents on a string of super-macho guy flicks (granted, he is super-sexy teamed with John Travolta in *Face/Off*). Thankfully, Cage periodically returns to chick flick territory.

Meanwhile, Cage's personal life takes just as many twists and turns. After divorcing first wife, Patricia Arquette (who also comes from a show biz family), he married Elvis Presley's daughter, Lisa Marie. After much drama, they, too, divorced. Nic's chick flick happy ending would have him finding true love with another show biz brat—instead, the third Mrs. Cage is a waitress.

Prince Charming Double Feature:

- *Moonstruck* (1987)—Nic plays a crazed one-handed baker, and yet he's the sexiest thing on earth. He looks pretty spiffy in a tuxedo too.

- *Captain Corelli's Mandolin* (2001)—A wartime romance with Nic playing up his Italian roots. His love interest is Tom Cruise's onetime real-life squeeze, Penelope Cruz.

Fifth-Runner Up: John Cusack

He's the thinking woman's sex symbol, a perpetual nice guy who likes to pretend he's dark and complicated. While John Cusack's sister Joan excels at second banana roles (*Runaway Bride*, *Broadcast News*, and even her bro's *Grosse Pointe Blank*), John has firmly entrenched himself in leading man land ever since his star-turning role in *Say Anything*. Like a fictional hero, Cusack comes equipped with a best friend, actor Jeremy Piven, who also plays this same role in many of John's movies. Interestingly, Piven played Nicolas Cage's best friend in *Family Man* and wasn't as believable. Clearly, the true friendship between Jeremy and John makes a difference. The one thing Jeremy has not done (which any good movie best friend would do) is convince Cusack that some lucky lady is the perfect Mrs. Cusack. John has dated a series of women, including co-stars like Neve Campbell, but has yet to tie the knot.

Prince Charming Double Feature:

- *Say Anything* (1989)—A classic teenage romance with John Cusack as a lovesick underachiever determined to woo the Big Girl on Campus. Who can forget Cusack holding up the boom box to serenade Ione Skye? An A+ truly memorable romantic movie moment.

- *The Journey of Natty Gann* (1985)—A live-action Disney family movie in which young Cusack helps a 14-year-old girl (Meredith Salenger) with her Great Depression–era trek.

Honorable Mention: Johnny Depp

Like George Clooney, Johnny Depp first came to our attention via his heartthrob role in a popular dramatic television series. In Depp's case, he played an undercover detective in *21 Jump Street*. Like Brad Pitt, Johnny fights against his good looks on screen, often disappearing in extreme disguises (*Edward Scissorhands* and *Pirates of the Caribbean: The Curse of the Black Pearl* being two prime examples). Nevertheless, his innate sweetness and undimmed sex appeal shine through. Who else but Johnny Depp could play a real-life drug dealer in *Blow* and make the character a romantic hero?

After high-profile romances with actresses like Winona Ryder, Johnny Depp fell in love with French chanteuse Vanessa Paradis, had children with her, and now lives happily in France as a family man. Named *People*'s Sexiest Man Alive in 2003, we have high hopes that Johnny Depp's future will include more Don Juan roles.

Prince Charming Double Bill

- *Don Juan DeMarco* (1995)—The main romance belongs to Marlon Brando and Faye Dunaway, but Johnny is wonderful as a mental patient who believes he is Don Juan.

- *Benny & Joon* (1993)—Aidan Quinn is Benny and Mary Stuart Masterson of *Fried Green Tomatoes* and *Some Kind of Wonderful* is his mentally unstable sister Joon. Johnny disappears in his role as the Buster Keaton and Charlie Chaplin–worshiping loon who falls for Joon.

Prince Charming Emeritus: Kevin Costner

For many years, Kevin Costner was married to his college sweetheart, Cindy. Eschewing a fancy Beverly Hills mansion for a modest suburban existence, the Costners and their children pursued the kind of down-to-earth lifestyle Kevin personifies so well on screen. After he and his wife got divorced, Kevin seemed to founder without his family to anchor him. Whereas once upon a time you could always count on a Kevin Costner chick flick to be top drawer, his post-divorce output has been uneven. You just know *Dragonfly* would have been much better if it had been made during his family man years.

Prince Charming Double Bill

- *The Bodyguard* (1992)—Kevin puts his life on the line for diva Whitney Houston. The bodyguard role was originally written for Steve McQueen, and Kevin honors this legacy with a McQueenesque hairstyle.

- *Message in a Bottle* (1999)—Costner's in love with his dead wife in this adaptation of a Nicholas Sparks novel. Paul Newman plays Kev's dad, and *The Princess Bride*'s Robin Wright Penn is his potential new love.

Prince Charming of All Time: Cary Grant

Move aside, all you pretenders. The undisputed king of chick flicks is Cary Grant. Cary Grant could do it all—action, romance, Hitchcock thrillers, physical comedy, etc.—and like our contemporary hunks, he always brought his own persona to the role. In the modern era, no leading man's cinematic output equals Grant's extensive roster of classic chick flicks, and only George Clooney comes close to equaling Grant's effortless charm.

In his personal life, Cary Grant lived like a dashing chick flick hero. He had a best friend with whom he roomed during his salad days, the impossibly handsome actor Randolph Scott. And although rumors swirled about their friendship, Grant spent decades marrying female after female. His grand total doesn't quite live up to Liz Taylor standards, but it's impressive: five. One was even a famous heiress (Barbara Hutton). Very late in life, he had his first child, Jennifer Grant, with wife number four, actress Dyan Cannon. His daughter became an actress and had a recurring role on *Beverly Hills, 90210*.

Prince Charming Double Feature:

- *Charade* (1963)—When Audrey Hepburn's husband is murdered, she turns to Cary Grant for help in this stylish thriller. *Charade* was remade as *The Truth about Charlie* in 2002. Director Jonathan Demme originally wanted Will Smith to fill Cary's shoes. Instead, Mark Wahlberg ended up not quite measuring up to the great man's mark.

- *To Catch a Thief* (1955)—Cary Grant is the thief, and Grace Kelly is the dame doing the catching. In real life, Miss Kelly snared the Prince of Monaco soon after making this Hitchcock romantic comedy-thriller. If you can't have Cary Grant, you might as well marry a real prince, right?

CHAPTER 7

The Hall of Fame
Ten Deserving Inductees

The Baseball Hall of Fame is located in Cooperstown, New York, and the Rock and Roll Hall of Fame can be found in Cleveland, Ohio. So where exactly is the Chick Flick Hall of Fame? In your home entertainment center. Yes, you are the curator of this highly prestigious organization, and you are in charge of inducting new members. Who shall you deem worthy to join your personal viewing library? Which films have the necessary star power, remarkable characterizations, unique story lines, memorable dialogue, impressive wardrobe, noteworthy set decoration, and killer soundtracks to make your cut? If you've just opened your doors and don't know which films to include, take a look at these ten candidates worthy of induction in any chick flick hall of fame. But as always, worthiness is a matter of opinion. While many consider *Pretty Woman* the ultimate modern-day chick flick, the (male) owner of the *Rank-o-Vision.com* Web site dismisses it as, "Some whore gets to stay with some rich guy for a week. Then she gets attacked by George Costanza." Clearly it wouldn't be making his Hall of Fame.

NUMBER 10:

The Way We Were

(1973)

Rated: PG

Cast: Barbra Streisand, Robert Redford, James Woods

Director: Sydney Pollack

Barbra Streisand plays an ugly duckling radical who nevertheless manages to mate with male swan Robert Redford; the film follows several decades of their off-and-on relationship. Because it's a tearjerker, we know she's not going to get to keep him, but it's glorious while it lasts. Although there has always been talk of a sequel to *The Way We Were*, reuniting the Streisand and Redford characters would invalidate this film's perfect ending. When the still politically radical Babs runs into Bob and his glamorous new "girl" on the street, your heart always breaks.

The Way We Were is hereby inducted into The Ultimate Guide to Chick Flicks Hall of Fame in honor of its complicated portrait of an ugly duckling heroine and unrequited love.

NUMBER 9:

Sense and Sensibility

(1995)

Rated: PG

Cast: Hugh Grant, Emma Thompson, Alan Rickman, Kate Winslet, Greg Wise

Director: Ang Lee

Star Emma Thompson adapted this Jane Austen novel and won an Academy Award for her effort. A little long in the tooth to be believable as a marriageable spinster, Ms. Thompson nevertheless is wonderful as the sensible Elinor while *Titanic's* Kate Winslet glows as her extravagantly emotional sister Marianne. Like the Gwyneth Paltrow version of Austen's *Emma*, this extremely well-produced and entertaining Hollywood production is star packed. Hugh Grant is the object of one sister's affection, Alan Rickman the kindly neighbor suffering in silent admiration for the other. Greg Wise, the lesser-known actor picked to portray the romantic cad Kate Winslet lusts after, must be just as irresistible in real life as he is on screen because Emma Thompson hooked up with him offscreen—and they're now married with child.

Sense and Sensibility is hereby inducted into The Ultimate Guide to Chick Flicks Hall of Fame in honor of its pitch-perfect adaptation of an Austen classic.

NUMBER 8
Shakespeare in Love
(1998)

Rated: R

Cast: Joseph Fiennes, Gwyneth Paltrow, Colin Firth, Ben Affleck, Judi Dench, Rupert Everett

Director: John Madden

As much as we enjoy the wonderful cinematic adaptations of *Romeo and Juliet*, we delight even more in this fictionalization of William Shakespeare's struggle to write that great masterpiece. Who knew that Will originally was going to title it *Romeo and Ethel, the Pirate's Daughter*? Even the most casual fan of Shakespeare's work will get the majority of references that populate this witty comedy. Ralph Fiennes's handsome

younger brother Joseph smolders as the blocked writer, and Gwyneth Paltrow won an Oscar for her portrayal of his sexy muse. Colin Firth takes on the bad boyfriend role as the man Paltrow is supposed to marry. Gwen's beau at the time, Ben Affleck, has a terrific supporting role as hammy actor.

Shakespeare in Love is hereby inducted into The Ultimate Guide to Chick Flicks Hall of Fame in honor of its witty new angle on a classic love story.

NUMBER 7:

Beaches

(1988)

Rated: PG-13

Cast: Bette Midler, Barbara Hershey, John Heard, Mayim Bialik

Director: Garry Marshall

Beaches is a story of two girls—one beautiful and rich, the other brash and poor—who meet by the seashore as children and experience an extremely complicated and intertwined friendship over the years. While it's pretty common for chick flicks to begin with a childhood prologue establishing crucial facts  about their adult main characters (*Broadcast News* does it wonderfully), preteen Mayim Bialik proved to be so outstanding as a young Bette Midler that she was rewarded with her own sitcom (*Blossom*). Based on a novel by Iris Rainer Dart and directed by *Pretty Woman*'s Garry Marshall, *Beaches* is an A+ tearjerker. Nevertheless, the movie maintains a wonderfully lighthearted tone as the two best friends suffer through many heartbreaks and betrayals before death darkens their doorstep.

Beaches is hereby inducted into The Ultimate Guide to Chick Flicks Hall of Fame in honor of its multi-layered depiction of female friendship.

NUMBER 6:

Steel Magnolias

(1989)

Rated: PG

Cast: Sally Field, Dolly Parton, Shirley MacLaine, Daryl Hannah, Olympia Dukakis, Julia Roberts

Director: Herbert Ross

First there was the play, created by a struggling actor, Robert Harling, who didn't know what to write about until he began jotting down some memories of his late sister and the community where they grew up. The beauty parlor–set stage play was so successful that it became a movie with an all-star cast. Although an ensemble piece, the emotional focus of this story is Sally Field, making that aging leading lady transition from headlining in gritty films like *Norma Rae* to playing "mother" roles. Co-star Shirley MacLaine is another example of a diva sliding into spicy supporting role territory after being the main attraction in *Sweet Charity* and *The Apartment*. Then there's Dolly Parton, the country singer famous for her blonde wigs and big bust, who is completely believable as Truvy, the small-town beauty shop owner (although, oddly, not so believable as Sam Shepard's wife). Daryl Hannah, who played a sex symbol mermaid only a few years earlier in *Splash*, downplays her looks to portray Dolly's timid fellow beautician. And of course there's Julia Roberts, a fairly brand-new ingenue starring as Sally Field's headstrong diabetic daughter, Julia Roberts determined to have a child to save her marriage even if it might kill her.

Steel Magnolias is hereby inducted into The Ultimate Guide to Chick Flicks Hall of Fame in honor of its stellar ensemble storytelling, centered around a gripping mother/daughter relationship.

NUMBER 5:
Sleepless in Seattle
(1993)

Rated: PG

Cast: Meg Ryan, Tom Hanks, Bill Pullman, Rosie O'Donnell, Rob Reiner

Director: Nora Ephron

Although they had previously starred together in *Joe Versus the Volcano*, this is the flick that cemented Tom Hanks and Meg Ryan as *the* romantic comedy couple of the modern chick flick era. Tom is a charming widower getting back into the dating scene with the encouragement of his best friend Rob Reiner (the real-life director of another Chick Flicks Hall of Famer, *When Harry Met Sally . . .*). His young son, however, has other plans. The little lad calls a radio talk show, allowing Meg and the rest of America to hear every detail about his father's sad story. Although engaged to Bill Pullman, Meg becomes obsessed with the man known to radio listeners as Sleepless in Seattle. It's not until their grand reunion at the top of the Empire State building (a rendezvous spot inspired by the film *An Affair to Remember*) that Tom and Meg formally meet face to face.

Sleepless in Seattle is hereby inducted into The Ultimate Guide to Chick Flicks Hall of Fame in honor of its unique twist on the standard "boy meets girl, boy loses girl, boy gets girl" scenario.

NUMBER 4:
When Harry Met Sally . . .
(1989)

Rated: R

Cast: Billy Crystal, Meg Ryan, Carrie Fisher, Bruno Kirby

Director: Rob Reiner

When Harry Met Sally . . . is a thoughtful meditation on a deep philosophical quandary: Can men and women ever be just friends? In the movie, Billy Crystal says no, sex is always part of the equation. He and Meg Ryan, both suffering from painful breakups, forge a fragile friendship while searching for new potential mates. When they ultimately fall into bed together, they overreact, fearing that sex will ruin everything. Their final revelation is that they can be lovers as well as friends. Although this film is chockful of memorable movie moments, it will be forever remembered for Meg's extremely public demonstration of how easy it is for women to fake orgasms.

When Harry Met Sally . . . is hereby inducted into The Ultimate Guide to Chick Flicks Hall of Fame in honor of its in-depth examination of the friends-versus-lovers question—and its classic orgasm in the deli scene.

Gone with the Wind

(1939)

Rated: G

Cast: Clark Gable, Vivien Leigh, Leslie Howard, Olivia de Havilland, Butterfly McQueen

Director: Victor Fleming

Is there any character in American literature who can hold a candle to Scarlett O'Hara? And how lucky are we that David O. Selznick risked casting a Brit to play her on the big screen? Vivien Leigh is impossibly marvelous as a Southern belle determined to do things her own way, the Union army and Clark Gable's Rhett Butler be damned. While few chick flicks can successfully carry a story line for more than an hour and a half, Scarlett's Civil War adventure has been holding audiences captive for 233 minutes for over half a century.

Gone with the Wind is hereby inducted into The Ultimate Guide to Chick Flicks Hall of Fame in honor of its incomparable feisty heroine.

NUMBER 2:
Breakfast at Tiffany's

(1961)

Rated: Not Rated

Cast: Audrey Hepburn, George Peppard, Patricia Neal, Buddy Ebsen, Martin Balsam, Mickey Rooney

Director: Blake Edwards

What motion picture character is more glamorous than Audrey Hepburn's Holly Golightly, with her streaked hair, dark glasses, and omnipresent little black dress? Holly's enviable wardrobe is an impressive achievement when you realize her only guaranteed source of income is paid visits to a jailed gangster. Reportedly writer Truman Capote created the Golightly persona with Marilyn Monroe in mind (how odd to think of Holly as a blowsy blonde). The revelation that Ms. G. was once a country bumpkin's teenage bride would have made more sense with Monroe, but who cares? We'll take Audrey any day. While very few female characters become iconic, Hepburn's Holly Golightly is in a class by herself.

Breakfast at Tiffany's is hereby inducted into The Ultimate Guide to Chick Flicks Hall of Fame in honor of its fashion icon status.

NUMBER 1:

Pretty Woman

(1990)

Rated: R

Cast: Richard Gere, Julia Roberts, Laura San Giacomo, Jason Alexander

Director: Garry Marshall

As popular as it is controversial, *Pretty Woman* is the story of a Hollywood hooker who is paid three thousand dollars to sleep with a ruthless businessman. Thanks to Julia Roberts's sexual healing, Richard Gere's beast of a billionaire becomes a better man. As for his contributions to her well-being, the highlight of the entire film is their shopping spree on Rodeo Drive. When the snooty Beverly Hills saleswomen snub our Julia (the female equivalent of being beaten up in the schoolyard), here comes her credit-card-brandishing hero to the rescue. An A+ memorable movie moment.

While the fairy tale of *Cinderella* has been molding young girls' romantic expectations for centuries, responsible adults worry that *Pretty Woman* is not suitable fodder for impressionable young minds. Give the little girls credit for recognizing that *Pretty Woman* resonates on many levels. "Vivian is a real victim of time and circumstances," patiently explains star Julia Roberts, theorizing why so many females relate to her character. "Though she's got a good heart and plenty of spirit, she's been beaten down for a long time. As the story evolves and she discovers more about Edward [Richard Gere's character], she also rediscovers her own finer qualities and experiences deep emotional and physical changes. *Pretty Woman* is really about two people who are very similar. They're both business people; they both make deals. That's how they contend with the world. It's about finding love in unexpected places." Costar Richard Gere adds, "I think the beauty of this story is watching them both (Edward and Vivian) escape and expand their respective worlds. When these two people meet, they discover a new and private world of communication and love—and possibility." What's so wrong about that?

How to justify this film to those who still can't accept the hooker premise? The ending says it all: Richard Gere rescues Julia Roberts from life on the street, but she rescues him too—emotionally and spiritually.

Pretty Woman is hereby inducted into the Ultimate Guide to Chick Flicks Hall of Fame in honor of its controversial spin on the Cinderella/Prince Charming scenario.

CHAPTER 8

Comfort Flicks

Favorites to View While Eating Ice Cream

What is the movie-watching equivalent of donning comfy sweat-pants, putting your hair up in a ponytail, and eating Ben & Jerry's Cherry Garcia straight out of the carton? Indulging in one of those reliable comfort flicks you pop into the VCR when you just want to relax. These tried-and-true favorites are old friends who keep you company when you're home alone and make you feel better when you're suffering from what Holly Golightly calls the mean reds. You've seen them at least twenty times, and yet you enjoy them every single time. And the amazing thing is most of them don't star any of the main-stays of chick flick superstardom. No Julia, no Hugh, no Nic, no Drew. Just amazing actor/actress pairings that come together for one magical romance. Go ahead, indulge.

Flick to View:
The American President
(1995)

ICE CREAM:
BEN & JERRY'S CHERRY GARCIA

In macho guy flicks, the president of the United States is usually stressed out about hostile aliens landing or highly trained assassins infiltrating the White House. In *The American President*, the leader of the free world's most pressing concern is scoring a dinner date. Annette Bening plays a comely lobbyist who catches the eye of the widowed Michael Douglas, who is more handsome than any real-life president since JFK. Many romantic comedies claim to be in the Tracy and Hepburn *Adam's Rib/Woman of the Year/Desk Set* vein, but *The American President* really is. Can't you see Spencer and Kate tackling the roles in an earlier era? It's also nice to see a middle-aged male lead partnered with a woman who is age-appropriate. Although there are subplots involving both characters' careers, politics doesn't get in the way of the romance. This film was written by Aaron Sorkin, who created the acclaimed television series *West Wing*, and directed by Rob Reiner, who also helmed *The Princess Bride* and *When Harry Met Sally . . .* , so you know you're in capable hands.

Alternate Politically Inclined Love Stories to View:

- *Maid in Manhattan* (2002)—Political hopeful Ralph Fiennes romances Jennifer Lopez, unaware that she's his hotel chambermaid.

- *Running Mates* (1992)—Senator Ed Harris's sweetie, children's book author Diane Keaton, has a radical past that could result in his political doom.

- *Speechless* (1994)—Michael Keaton and Geena Davis are speechwriters who fall in love on the campaign trail while working for opposing candidates.

Flick to View:
The Cutting Edge
(1992)

ICE CREAM:
BASKIN-ROBBINS MINT CHOCOLATE CHIP

The truth is most sports flicks contain sappy stories that somehow tap into issues that guys find incredibly moving. Extremely macho men will swear to you that *The Rookie*, for example, is one of the best films ever made. While you can enjoy watching that Dennis Quaid baseball yarn with your fella, it won't speak to you the same way it does to him. Luckily, there are a few sports sagas designed to appeal to us chicks. In *The Cutting Edge*, D. B. Sweeney is a hockey player sidelined by an injury and forced to team up with a snooty figure skater with Olympic dreams. Moira Kelly plays the soon-to-be-melted ice maiden. This battle-of-the-sexes romance becomes an all-time favorite for every chick flick enthusiast who discovers it.

Alternate Sporty Flicks to View:

- *Ice Castles* (1978)—Another ice-skating romance, with Lynn-Holly Johnson as the blind skater and Robby Benson as the man who loves her. Some enthusiasts prefer *Ice Castles* to *The Cutting Edge*. Watch both and make your own decision.

- *Bend It Like Beckham* (2003)—Two English girls are crazy about soccer. In case you were worried the movie might veer too far away from chick flick territory, there's an extended subplot about a wedding. Beckham, by the way, is the Michael Jordan of soccer, and he and his Mrs. (a Spice Girl formerly known as Posh) make a very quick cameo in the film.

- *Blue Crush* (2002)—Kate Bosworth is a Hawaii-based hotel maid who also happens to be an athlete in training for a major surf competition. She almost gives up her Hang Ten dreams when she falls hard for a rich hunk staying at the hotel.

Flick to View:
The English Patient
(1996)

ICE CREAM:
MCCONNELL'S ENGLISH TOFFEE

While Ralph Fiennes famously played an evil Nazi in *Schindler's List*, in this particular World War II saga, he'd rather be a lover than a fighter. Based on Michael Ondaatje's novel, *The English Patient* uses flashbacks to reveal what has led up to Fiennes's status as a burn victim being cared for by Juliette Binoche. Turns out he's a cartographer in love with Colin Firth's wife, Kristin Scott Thomas. While there are several story lines going on in this clever Oscar-winning film, you can't help but focus your attention on Ralph and Kristin's doomed romance. Get out your handkerchiefs, it's a tearjerker.

Alternate Wartime Romances to View:

- *A Town Like Alice* (1981)—In this Australian television miniseries available on DVD, a plucky group of women are taken prisoners of war by the Japanese during World War II. Bryan Brown is a hunky Aussie soldier who tries to help them out.

- *Cold Mountain* (2003)—During the Civil War, rebel soldier Jude Law goes AWOL to return home to his true love, the destitute but still glamorous Nicole Kidman.

- *Swing Shift* (1984)—While her husband is away fighting in World War II, sheltered California housewife Goldie Hawn joins the home front workforce. Getting a job in a factory, she ultimately hooks up with coworker/musician Kurt Russell.

Flick to View:
Flashdance
(1983)

ICE CREAM:
DREYER'S GRAND LIGHT ROCKY ROAD

Any movie where the lead character is a welder by day and an exotic dancer by night is going to be mocked by serious cineastes. Those film snobs don't know what they're missing. Jennifer Beals, who plays the plucky steelworker with ballerina aspirations, did not do her own footwork. Nevertheless, she looks stunning as a dancer, and her ripped sweatshirt and legwarmers have become a movie costume icon. In fact, Jennifer Lopez is such a fan of the look that she imitated it for her music video, "I'm Glad."

Alternate Aspiring Dancers Sagas to View:

- *Center Stage* (2000) —*Flashdance* ended with Jennifer Beals being accepted into the Pittsburgh Academy of Dance. If there had been a sequel following her adventure, it might have been something like this ballet school drama. Look for American Ballet Theatre star Ethan Stiefel as the bad boy worshipped by good girl Amanda Schull.

- *Coyote Ugly* (2000)—More girls dancing in bars, but these fillies are actually tending bar while hotfooting.

- *Save the Last Dance* (2001)—*Flashdance* for the MTV generation. Julia Stiles is the latest in a cinematic line of misfits who get the boy of their dreams while shaking a tail feather. In this case, hip hop moves are required to win over her urban hero.

Flick to View:
Gentlemen Prefer Blondes
(1953)

ICE CREAM:
DAIRY QUEEN SOFT-SERVE VANILLA

Marilyn Monroe and Jane Russell star as two showgirls who board an ocean cruiser bound for (in dumb blonde Marilyn's words) "France, Paris." While Jane is attracted to poor boys, Marilyn is obsessed with rich men. The film is packed with gold-digger wisdom, such as Marilyn's theory that a man being rich is like a woman being pretty—not absolutely necessary, but it doesn't hurt! The film's musical numbers ("Diamonds

Are a Girl's Best Friend") are also classic, and the courtroom scene where Jane Russell puts on a platinum wig and pretends to be Marilyn is a hoot.

Alternate Gold-Digger Gems to View:

- *How to Marry a Millionaire* (1953)—Marilyn stars as another blonde out to hook a fellow with big bucks. This time around, her best friends are fellow millionaire-hunters Betty Grable and Lauren Bacall. All three are models, so you know you're in for a fabulous fashion show.

- *Overboard* (1987)—A reverse gold-digger comedy. Goldie Hawn stars as a rich bitch who falls off her yacht, loses her memory, and finds happiness as the poor wife of Kurt Russell.

- *Gold Diggers of 1935* (1935)—A backstage romance featuring a rich widow, a con man, and a blackmailer, this glorious Busby Berkeley musical culminates in the awe-inspiring "Lullaby of Broadway" production number. Look for actress Gloria Stuart, who six decades later would play the present-day version of Kate Winslet's Rose in *Titanic*.

Flick to View:
Grease
(1978)

ICE CREAM:
CARNATION NEAPOLITAN ICE CREAM BAR

Welcome to Fifties-era Rydell High. Australian songbird Olivia Newton-John is Sandy, a good girl who discovers that if she wants to win the true love of bad boy John Travolta she's got to tart herself up. Olivia hangs out with a female gang called The Pink Ladies, while John and his buddies dance up a storm during shop class. Everyone in the movie is clearly way too old to be playing teenagers, but somehow it's all just wonderful. Note: *Grease* spawned a 1982 sequel, *Grease 2*, for which Travolta and Newton-John declined to return; so the second time around the heroine (Michelle Pfeiffer) is the cool one and the hero (Maxwell Caulfield) the innocent foreigner.

Alternate Poodle Skirt/Leather Jacket Couplings to View:

- *Bye Bye Birdie* (1963)—Inspired by Elvis Presley's 1958 induction into the army, this light and bubbly musical showcases Ann-Margret as a lucky teenage fan club president chosen to give her army-bound idol one last televised kiss on *The Ed Sullivan Show*.

- *Gidget* (1959)—Sandra Dee (the ultimate 1950s good girl blonde) shines as a "girl midget" who worships a hunky beach bum nicknamed Moondoggie.

- *Cry-Baby* (1990)—Bad boy Johnny Depp sings (and cries) in director John Waters's retro homage to fifties juvenile delinquent rock and roll melodramas.

Flick to View:
Now and Then
(1995)

ICE CREAM:
SNICKERS WITH ALMONDS
ICE CREAM BAR

Four women who were best friends as preteens in the seventies reunite when one of them is about to give birth. The hometown reunion sparks many memories of their not-so-carefree childhood and the summer that changed them forever. What amazing casting: Demi Moore and her pre-teen counterpart Gabby Hoffmann, Rosie O'Donnell and Christina Ricci, Melanie Griffith and Thora Birch, and Rita Wilson (Mrs. Tom Hanks) and Ashleigh Aston Moore.

Alternate Female Ensemble Pieces to View:

- *Waiting to Exhale* (1995)—An A+ novel turned into a stellar movie, Terry McMillan's story follows the trials and tribulations of four Phoenix-based women suffering from man troubles. The exhalers are Whitney Houston, Angela Bassett, Loretta Devine, and Lela Rochon.

- *Divine Secrets of the Ya-Ya Sisterhood* (2002)—Based on the fabulous novel about a group of lifelong friends, the Ya-Ya secrets are told in flashbacks. Ashley Judd plays the ringleader Vivi as a young woman, while Ellen Burstyn embodies her today.

- *The Women* (1939)—Talk about an all-female ensemble piece; in this movie about the repercussions of an extramarital affair, no men appear on screen. The all-star cast features Norma Shearer, Joan Crawford, Rosalind Russell, and Paulette Goddard.

Flick to View:
Somewhere in Time
(1980)

ICE CREAM:
STARBUCKS COFFEE JAVA CHIP

Before he broke his neck in a riding accident, but after he played Superman, Christopher Reeve starred in this romantic fantasy about a modern-day playwright who becomes obsessed with an actress from 1912. Before she played Dr. Quinn Medicine Woman on TV, Jane Seymour used her glorious long locks to mesmerize Reeve, who goes back to 1912 to romance her. How does this time travel happen? By self-hypnosis. And unlike the unthinking travelers who typically populate sci fi flicks, Christopher makes sure he dresses appropriately before arriving (although the joke's on him because the outfit he scored from a vintage dealer is out of date by 1912). The Grand Hotel where the majority of the action takes place is so irresistible that you'll pick Michigan's Mackinac Island as your next getaway vacation spot.

Alternate Time-Bending Tales to View:

- *The French Lieutenant's Woman* (1981)—Lovers Jeremy Irons and Meryl Streep exist in two different time periods as they portray modern actors acting out scenes in a costume period drama.

- *Kate & Leopold* (2001)—Dashing English duke Hugh Jackman travels forward in time and lands on Meg Ryan's contemporary doorstep. How can anyone resist Hugh Jackman in a romance novel concept come to life?

- *Possession* (2002)—Based on an A. S. Byatt novel, this drama is a treat for hardcore fans of Austen adaptations: Modern-day scholars Gwyneth Paltrow (star of 1996's *Emma*) and Aaron Eckhart research the historical romance of nineteenth-century poets Jennifer Ehle (who played Elizabeth in 1995's *Pride and Prejudice*) and Jeremy Northam (Knightley in *Emma*).

Flick to View:
Strictly Ballroom
(1992)

ICE CREAM:
HÄAGEN-DAZS WHITE CHOCOLATE
RASPBERRY TRUFFLE

Want to know director Baz Luhrmann's dirty little secret? He was a ball-room dancer as a child. No wonder he knows the over-the-top world of Australian dance competitions so well. "Ballroom dancing allows anybody to fulfill a fantasy dream of glamour," he explains. "You can be working in a used-car lot during the day, and at night you can be the king or queen of the ballroom world. That's its magic." There's nothing better than watching hero Paul Mercurio slide on his knees across the dance floor to his formerly ugly duckling dance partner Tara Morice—wow! The *Strictly Ballroom* DVD includes *Samba to Slow Fox Dance*, a documentary on the Australian ballroom dance world. You'll be amazed to note that the real-life participants and their costumes aren't that far removed from the *Strictly Ballroom* creations.

Alternate Outrageous Aussie Escapades to View:

- *Muriel's Wedding* (1994)—With the help of her best friend Rachel Griffiths, Abba-loving Toni Collette escapes her nutty family and makes a new life for herself in Sydney. Warning: Tears will be shed.

- *The Adventures of Priscilla, Queen of the Desert* (1994)—Drag queens make their way across the Australian outback in a dilapidated bus they call Priscilla. Look for *Memento*'s Guy Pearce as the prettiest cross-dresser.

- *Starstruck* (1982)—A flashy teenage waitress and her younger brother have rock and roll dreams in this Gillian Armstrong–directed musical. If John Hughes had been an Aussie woman, he would have made this movie.

Flick to View:
White Palace

(1990)

ICE CREAM:
GODIVA VANILLA WITH
CHOCOLATE CARAMEL HEARTS

As the tagline on the video box promises, *White Palace* is "the story of a younger man and a bolder woman." James Spader plays an uptight widower who falls in love with a low-class waitress at least fifteen years his senior. Of course, she's played by the enduringly sexy Susan Sarandon, who certainly knows from her own experience with Tim Robbins that there's pleasure in loving a younger man.

Alternate May–December Teamings to View:

- *Tim* (1979)—Young Mel Gibson stars as a simple man who proves to be an older woman's unexpected prince charming. Piper Laurie plays the rich woman who falls for her pretty-faced yard worker. Based on a book by the author of *The Thornbirds*.

- *Something's Gotta Give* (2003)—Jack Nicholson only dates much younger women—until he meets his latest girlfriend's mother, Diane Keaton, who is also being romanced by Jack's young stud-muffin heart doctor, Keanu Reeves.

- *My First Mister* (2001)—Leelee Sobieski is a punky teen who gets a job in a men's clothing store working for fussy middle-aged neurotic Albert Brooks. The two misfits rub each other wrong at first but ultimately find they are well suited. Warning: It's a tearjerker.

CHAPTER 9

Special Editions

Seven Spectacular DVDs

Most chick flick devotees already have personal video copies of their favorites. After all, a good chick flick deserves to be watched time and time again. But what's a girl to do when her prized possessions are being reissued on a superior format—DVD? Some grand epics like *Gone with the Wind* or *Titanic* are definitely worth buying on DVD just because it's a crime not to see these visual masterpieces in the best possible format. Additionally, those longer films previously issued on two bulky VHS tapes are so much easier to store when they're contained on one slim disc. Ditto television miniseries like *Pride and Prejudice* or TV series like *Sex and the City*, *Friends*, *Gilmore Girls*, or *Buffy the Vampire Slayer*, which come in sleek multi-DVD cases. Of course, with DVD you have the added benefit of chapter selections, which allows you to jump immediately to your favorite scenes—no more wasting time fast-forwarding. And if you bring your laptop computer or portable DVD player with you on business trips, you'll never ever again have to sit through those terrible airplane movies. A flight to Paris seems like it's over within minutes if you bring along your favorite French flicks.

While you don't need to replace your entire collection, there are dozens of DVDs well worth the price of acquisition. This sample group of seven spectacular DVDs offers so many extras that you have a whole new appreciation of stories you thought you knew by heart.

Amélie
(2001)

In the great tradition of showing Paris at its most romantic, *Amélie* is the best movie to come out of France since, well, this century began! Not only does star Audrey Tautou share the same first name as the late-lamented Audrey Hepburn, she's got gamine features equally as wonderful as her namesake's. Mademoiselle Tautou portrays Amélie, a fanciful Parisian waitress who discovers a hidden box full of some stranger's childhood mementos and decides to return the box to its rightful owner. This sets off a chain of delightful adventures in which she meddles in many people's lives. Star Audrey Tautou reports, "The story really touches some people and evokes a feeling of dreams. It isn't just a sweet film that you forget about after you've walked out of the theater. I don't think that there are many films that make you look at your life and the world around you the way *Amélie* does."

WHY YOU'LL LOVE THE DVD

First off, the film is in French, so you have to see it more than once to adequately enjoy the visuals without having to worry about reading subtitles. For that reason alone, you'd want to own the DVD. But the DVD offers so much more than the chance to watch this extremely fast-paced film over and over again. In addition to two commentaries from Jean-Pierre Jeunet (one in French and other in English, for those of us who do not parlez français like a native), special features include mini-docs: *The Look of* Amélie, *Inside the Making of* Amélie, and *Fantasies of Audrey Tautou* (charming flubs and outtakes); two Q&A's with the director, one including the cast; screen tests, including Audrey's; hairstyle tests with Audrey, photos of *The Garden Gnome's Travels*, and much more. A whole second disc is added just to contain all these special features. Best tidbit gleaned: Emily Watson of *Breaking the Waves* fame would have been cast as the title character if only she spoke French.

Fans of Amélie might enjoy these stylish foreign flicks:

- *Venus Beauty Institute* (1999)—Ms. Tautou is a supporting character in this French female ensemble flick set in a Parisian beauty salon.

- *Breathless (1961)*—This flick was groundbreaking in its day for its visual flash (MTV-style editing, decades before music videos even existed). Young Jean-Paul Belmondo and Jean Seberg are gloriously cast as a small-time crook and his American babe.

- *Run Lola Run* (1998)—If Amélie were a tough German babe with red hair and a bad boyfriend, you'd have Lola.

Dirty Dancing—Ultimate Edition
(1987)

Set in 1963, Jennifer Grey plays Frances "Baby" Houseman, a seventeen-year-old whose family always vacations in the Catskills. This magical summer, she escapes the planned activities that her older sister so enthusiastically embraces and slips away to grind pelvises with sexy dance instructor Johnny Castle (played by Patrick Swayze).

The late director Emile Ardolino is on record saying "Dirty dancing is the most erotic form of partner dancing. When people started dancing away from each other what was lost was the wonderful experience of taking someone in your arms and dancing cheek to cheek or hip to hip or shoulder to shoulder. Touching each other, communicating with each other, that's what dancing has always been. If two people are dancing, looking into each other's eyes and trying to convey, 'I love you,' that's the most intimate kind of communication, the most intimate outside of the bedroom."

Choreographer Kenny Ortega further clarifies for those who want to master the steps at home, "Dirty dancing is like soul dancing, only with a partner. A little Mambo is thrown in, a little Cuban motion, too, a conglomeration of rhythms and movements. And because it's soul dancing, it's something that comes out as an expression. It's not about technique as much as it is about feeling."

WHY YOU'LL LOVE THE DVD

There have been several special edition versions of *Dirty Dancing*. The latest version is called the Ultimate Edition, so we might be safe to assume it's the best. There are two commentary tracks, neither by the director since he passed away. The most interesting commentary is by screenwriter Eleanor Bergstein, who did dirty dancing as a teenager. (The other features a handful of key crew people including choreographer Kenny Ortega and his assistant choreographer Miranda Garrison, plus the director of photography, the costume director, and the production designer.) On a second disc, there are a variety of video interviews; the best one with Jennifer Grey. Jen is a wonderful gossip, sharing that she was "this close" to getting the lead in *Flashdance* and that she thought Billy Zane (the evil fiancé from *Titanic*) was going to get the role of Johnny in *Dirty Dancing*.

Jennifer's screen test (dramatic scenes, plus a quick dirty dance with choreographer Kenny Ortega) is a special feature, along with the full-length concert film Dirty Dancing: Live In Concert, three music videos ("She's Like the Wind," "Hungry Eyes," and "I've Had the Time of My Life"), the original theatrical trailer, and a quick look at the sequel, Dirty Dancing: Havana Nights (2004).

Fans of Dirty Dancing might enjoy these sexy summer romances:

- *A Walk on the Moon* (1999)—Diane Lane plays a housewife who hooks up with hunky Viggo Mortensen during the family vacation in the Catskills.

- *Little Darlings* (1980)—Teenage vixens Kristy McNichol and Tatum O'Neal find love at summer camp. Matt Dillon is the Johnny Castle–like bad boy. Look for a young blonde Cynthia Nixon (red-headed Miranda from *Sex and the City*) as a fellow camper.

- *Summer Lovers* (1982)—Peter Gallagher (the dad on *The O.C.*) is young and hunky in this drama about a young American couple who tryst in the Greek Islands with a sexy free spirit. Still looking very much like *Splash*'s mermaid, Daryl Hannah plays Gallagher's wife.

The Princess Bride—Special Edition
(1987)

The best thing about *The Princess Bride* is that it's the quintessential guy-friendly chick flick. The many action scenes might have something to do with the movie's heavy male appeal, although the fellas seem to enjoy the comedy bits as well. *The Princess Bride* also plays well to small children.

After all, it was originally conceived to entertain the author's daughters. "I'll write you a story," author William Goldman promised them. "What do you want it to be about?" One daughter said princesses, the other brides, so Goldman melded the two requests. By the way, if you haven't read Goldman's original book, you absolutely must—it's just as charming as the film.

Robin Wright (who would later add Penn to her name when she married Madonna's ex) loves studly farmhand/pirate Cary Elwes (who had the potential to be the British Brad Pitt but somehow never became a star), yet she is promised to evil prince Chris Sarandon (Susan's ex). After a lot of swordplay, she ends up with the correct guy.

WHY YOU'LL LOVE THE DVD

In addition to the two commentaries (one by director Rob Reiner, the second by author William Goldman), there's a slew of documentaries and featurettes, including *Cary Elwes' Video Diary* (behind-the-scenes shot by Cary himself during production). The DVD also comes with a glossy six-page booklet.

Fans of The Princess Bride might enjoy these:

- *Naughty Marietta* (1935)—A flick that your grandmother probably loved. Jeanette MacDonald and Nelson Eddy star in this old-fashioned musical about a bride captured by pirates.

- *A Knight's Tale* (2001)—Hunky Aussie star Heath Ledger plays a fourteenth-century knight who jousts, hangs out with a totally naked poet named Chaucer, and yet dances to the music of contemporary artists.

- *Lady Jane* (1986)—Cary Elwes once again romances a royal beauty, this time in a serious costume drama. Helena Bonham

Carter plays a fifteen-year-old who becomes queen of England for a very brief period in 1553.

A Room with a View—Two Disc Special Edition
(1985)

Based on the E. M. Forster novel, this Merchant-Ivory production features Helena Bonham Carter as a virginal Englishwoman traveling in Italy who escapes her female companions to hook up with fellow Englishman Julian Sands. Julian shows Helena a thing or two about passion, but then she has to return to England and her stuffy bad boyfriend, Daniel Day-Lewis. Rupert Graves is charming as Helena's brother, and there's a scene where the neighborhood men romp around a pond in complete full frontal nudity.

WHY YOU'LL LOVE THE DVD

Did I mention there's a scene where men romp around nude? Since *A Room with a View* was originally released on DVD with no extra features, the 2004 Special Edition (two discs) is highly welcomed. In addition to a refurbished film transfer and soundtrack, there's now commentary by Merchant, Ivory, and gabby actor Simon Callow (who plays the Reverend Mr. Beebe). Special features include clips from British talk show promotional appearances made by Callow and Daniel Day-Lewis during the film's original theatrical release, a 1985 BBC news story about the film's appeal to American moviegoers, and an E. M. Forster documentary made shortly after the author's death. A photo gallery of never-before-seen images rounds out the new goodies.

Fans of A Room with a View might enjoy these Forster adaptations:

- *Howards End* (1992)—Helena Bonham Carter does Forster once more. This time she's cast as Emma Thompson's sister. Anthony Hopkins is the rich man who worships the less fortunate Emma and eventually marries her when wife Vanessa Redgrave dies.

- *Where Angels Fear to Tread* (1991)—Helena Bonham Carter is once again in Italy, but this flick focuses on Helen Mirren and her romance with a much younger man.

- *A Passage to India* (1984)—Directed by the great David Lean, Judy Davis stars as a British woman who causes trouble when she accuses an Indian doctor of a terrible crime.

The Sound of Music—Collector's Edition
(1965)

Whether you're sixteen going on seventeen or sixty going on seventy, you'll always have a weakness for this family favorite. Unable to fit in with the other novices at the convent, wannabe nun Julie Andrews is sent to be a governess for the seven children of a stern widowed Austrian war hero (Christopher Plummer). Thanks to her sunny disposition and catchy songs, Julie wins the children's hearts, but Plummer is under the mistaken impression that the right woman for him is blonde bombshell baroness Eleanor Parker. Plummer realizes his mistake, and the family escapes the Nazis by singing their way across the Salzburg mountains.

WHY YOU'LL LOVE THE DVD

This special two-disc DVD comes in a lovely package, which includes a glossy booklet. There are trailers and TV ads, commentary by director Robert Wise, audio interviews with screenwriter Ernest Lehman, and an extensive photo gallery. One of the most exciting bonus features is a mini-doc made during the original production called *Salzburg Sight and Sound*. It's a tour of the city (complete with a behind-the-scenes visit to the set) starring the actress who played the sixteen-year-old Liesl, Charmian Carr. The other amazing special feature is *The Sound of Music: From Fact to Phenomenon*, a much longer documentary that covers the history of the real-life von Trapps.

Fans of The Sound of Music might also enjoy these Julie A. faves:

- *Mary Poppins* (1964)—Who else could portray a singing governess/nanny who is practically perfect in every way?

- *The Princess Diaries* (2001)—Miss Andrews takes on the role of a royal grandmother training a stubborn American teenager to be princess in this film and the sequel *The Princess Diaries 2: Royal Engagement* (2004).

- *Eloise at the Plaza* (2003)—Guess who plays Eloise's singing nanny in this live action, musical version of the beloved children's classic. Fear not, that horrid hairstyle is a wig, and the impressive rump is wardrobe padding.

Thelma & Louise —Special Edition
(1991)

Thelma and Louise have become such strong figures in the pop culture landscape, it's hard to believe they didn't always exist. "I got the idea while sitting in my car outside of my house one night," reveals screenwriter Callie Khouri. "What could possibly happen in the lives of two women, two best friends, that would force them to choose between what they had and what they might be able to have? What one event, what mistake perhaps, would make them journey into the unknown? From there the story just started rolling out."

In the movie, best friends Geena Davis (Thelma) and Susan Sarandon (Louise) get into trouble when Susan shoots a barfly who is sexually mauling Geena. On the lam, they pick up sexy hitchhiker Brad Pitt, are hunted down by nice guy cop Harvey Keitel, and ultimately drive their T-bird off a cliff. *Thelma & Louise* creator Callie Khouri clarifies, "As a person, I truly believe that you get more than one shot in life. Thelma and Louise's road trip, if you will, is really a passage to some greater journey. As they turn each corner on the highway, they take one more step toward a way of life they never thought they could have—a life where they truly make their own decisions and, in the end, are happier for it."

WHY YOU'LL LOVE THE DVD

In addition to the two great commentaries (one by director Ridley Scott, the other by Susan Sarandon, Geena Davis, and writer Callie Khouri), this two-disc set offers a major documentary, *Thelma & Louise: The Last Journey.* The doc features interviews done in 2001 with Susan Sarandon,

Geena Davis, Michael Madsen (Louise's boyfriend), director Ridley Scott, writer Callie Khouri, and most impressively Brad Pitt (who admits his "soldier" saluted in his bedroom scene with Geena Davis). There's another featurette, made at the time of production, which includes a lot of behind-the-scenes footage. And if that isn't enough, there are also thirty minutes of newly found deleted/extended scenes, which include more of Brad Pitt and the extended alternate ending (with director's commentary). However, don't get too excited: there isn't that much more of Pitt and the alternate ending merely shows a little more footage of the T-bird flying farther into the canyon.

Fans of Thelma & Louise might enjoy these dynamic duos:

- *Butch Cassidy and the Sundance Kid* (1969)—The male version of *Thelma & Louise*, with old-school hunks Paul Newman and Robert Redford as the title characters. These two macho outlaws also choose to throw themselves into a deadly situation with reckless abandon when hunted down by an absurdly large police force.

- *Bound* (1996)—Think of it as a sexed-up, dumbed-down version of *Thelma & Louise*. Gina Gershon and Jennifer Tilly play two daring dames who seduce each other and steal two million dollars from the mob in this film noir written and directed by the Wachowski Brothers (who went on to create *The Matrix* trilogy).

- *The Piano* (1993)—Like Thelma and Louise, Holly Hunter and daughter Anna Paquin travel a great distance and encounter Harvey Keitel. Writer/director Jane Campion delivers a modern classic in this tale of a mute piano lover in nineteenth-century New Zealand.

Valley Girl—Special Edition
(1983)

In this Southern California tale of a pair of Romeo and Juliet–like star-crossed teenage lovers, Deborah Foreman plays the title character, a chipper blonde who dwells in the San Fernando Valley. Nicolas Cage is a Hollywood hipster who hates slang-spewing Valley girls. Naturally, they fall in love, much to the dismay of their fellow tribesmen.

Please note that Nicolas Cage was only seventeen years old (and freshly minted as Cage rather than Coppola) when he got the role of Randy. Already fiercely committed to altering his physicality for each role, he shaved his chest hair in the shape of a triangle to make Randy seem more "punk." Check out his handiwork in the beach scene.

WHY YOU'LL LOVE THE DVD

The featurette, *Valley Girl: 20 Totally Tubular Years Later*, has recent interviews with director Martha Coolidge, the producers/screenwriters, and most of the cast. An additional bonus piece, *In Conversation: Nicolas Cage and Martha Coolidge*, showcases the film's star and director informally chatting. A third mini-doc, *The Music of Valley Girl*, has new interviews with the soundtrack artists (The Plimsouls, Modern English, and Josie Cotton). Two vintage music videos (The Plimsouls' "A Million Miles Away" and Modern English's "I Melt with You") complete the package.

Fans of Valley Girl might also enjoy these I ❤ 1980s flicks:

- *Pretty in Pink* (1986) —Molly Ringwald loves popular pretty boy Andrew McCarthy, ignoring the fact that quirky best friend Jon Cryer adores her.

- *Can't Buy Me Love* (1987) —High school loser Patrick Dempsey pays a popular girl (Amanda Peterson) to make him over into a teen dream.

- *The Wedding Singer* (1998)—Adam Sandler loses what he thinks is his dream girl, but wins fellow wedding circuit vet Drew Barrymore in this period piece set in the Eighties. Look for punk rocker Billy Idol's cameo appearance (as himself).

CHAPTER 10

Hidden Treasures
An A-Z of Forgotten Films

You know what's wrong with the Meg Ryan/Tom Hanks romances? There are only three of them (so far). Same thing with the Doris Day/Rock Hudson classics. After you've burned through *Pillow Talk*, *Lover Come Back*, and *Send Me No Flowers*, what do you do? The answer is cast a wider net. These hidden treasures are flicks that you might be overlooking on your trip to the video store. Give 'em a shot. You won't be disappointed.

Ash Wednesday (1973)—Fans of plastic surgery reality shows like *The Swan* and *Extreme Makeover* will adore this stylish Elizabeth Taylor flick. Fearing her looks have deteriorated over the course of her thirty-year marriage to Henry Fonda, Liz heads to Italy for a face-lift (shown in gruesome detail). As the video box proclaims, "Surgery took years off her face, but can it save her marriage?" The restored Taylor, outfitted in glamorous Edith Head creations, must decide if she wants to return to her old life or pursue new options.

Bell Book and Candle (1958)—Stylish Kim Novak is art gallery owner Gillian Holroyd, a sexy blonde witch who resists using her magical powers in order to blend in with the mortals (shades of TV's *Bewitched*, n'est-ce pas?). Falling hard for new upstairs neighbor James Stewart, she casts a spell to steal him away from his bad girlfriend. When Stewart finds out Novak is a black magic woman, all hell breaks lose.

Cat Ballou (1965)—In this comedic musical western, sex kitten Jane Fonda is the title character, a spunky schoolmarm forced to hire gun-fighters to save her father's ranch from bad guys. Lee Marvin won an Os-car for playing two parts: the evil noseless Tim Strawn and the drunkard Kid Shelleen, who ultimately sobers up to save the day. Made on the cheap in little over a month, this Western spoof turned out to be one of the biggest box office hits of 1965. Thirty-three years later, the Farrelly brothers decided to use the *Cat Ballou* concept of on-screen balladeers (Nat King Cole and Stubby Kaye) in *There's Something About Mary* (Jonathan Richman).

Dogfight (1991)—The late River Phoenix plays a gung ho Marine with one night of R&R in San Francisco before shipping out for Vietnam. He and three buddies bolster their confidence by hosting a dogfight. As the video box taglines explain, "The rules of the dogfight were simple: every-one puts in fifty bucks. And the guy with the ugliest 'date' wins." River picks Lili Taylor, a gawky folk-singing waitress. A good guy at heart, River makes up for the dogfight by spending the rest of the night ro-mancing Lili.

Everyone Says I Love You (1996)—This is a musical where the stars do their own singing—and the stars are Julia Roberts, Drew Barrymore, Goldie Hawn, Edward Norton, Natalie Portman, Tim Roth, and Woody

Allen. Yes, it's a Woody Allen movie, set in New York, Venice, and Paris. The musical bits include Edward Norton doing endearingly amateurish Fred Astaire moves while buying Drew Barrymore an engagement ring at Harry Winston. Stay for the ending, a magical dance number where former hoofer Goldie Hawn literally flies along the banks of the Seine.

Foxes (1980)—Four fast Southern California high school girls are on the loose and at loose ends in this disco-era melodrama. Surprisingly, one of the foxes is Jodie Foster. This female *Saturday Night Fever* was directed by Adrian Lyne (helmer of *Flashdance*, *9 1/2 Weeks*, *Indecent Proposal*, and *Unfaithful*). TV hunk Scott Baio is the love interest, and Cherie Currie of the prototypical punk girl band The Runaways is Jodie's extremely messed up best friend. As the video box proudly highlights, the "hot" soundtrack is packed with hits from Boston, Donna Summer, and Cher.

Giant (1956)—Elizabeth Taylor is a Southern belle who takes one look at visiting Texan Rock Hudson and decides she must have him. In Texas, Ms. Taylor encounters major culture shock. Feeling like an outsider, she bonds with the local bad boy, played by the king of all bad boys, James Dean. Liz, Rock, and Jimmy (who died in car crash shortly thereafter) never looked more beautiful than they do in this sprawling epic love story.

Holiday (1938) —Fans of *The Philadelphia Story* will adore this earlier pairing of Katherine Hepburn and Cary Grant in a delightful romantic comedy by the same scribe. Once again Kate's the strong-willed daughter of a millionaire, and Cary thinks she's swell. The complication: He's just gotten engaged to her sister.

If a Man Answers (1962)—Real life sweeties Sandra Dee and Bobby Darin star in this Doris Day/Rock Hudson–esque piece of Sixties fluff. Bobby's a swinging bachelor fashion photographer tamed by good girl/

model Sandy. Worried that she can't keep Bobby's affection, Sandy employs a series of noteworthy man-catching techniques, such as having a pretend lover hang up every time Bobby answers the phone (hence the film's title). Think of it as *How to Lose a Guy in 10 Days*, in reverse.

Jailhouse Rock (1957)—Back when Elvis Presley was a rock and roll devil who drove the teenage girls wild by shaking his pelvis on *The Ed Sullivan Show*, Hollywood manufactured this rock and roll fable to showcase his talents. Judy Tyler plays the savvy record executive who believes in the ex-con's talent but resists falling in love with him.

Kissing Jessica Stein (2001)—Disappointed by bad boyfriends, Jessica Stein (Jennifer Westfeldt) makes a radical move: She answers a personal ad taken out by a woman (Heather Juergensen). This mainstream indie romantic comedy with a definite *Sex and the City* vibe was written by the two stars.

Love with the Proper Stranger (1963)—Department store salesgirl Natalie Wood has a one-night fling with musician Steve McQueen and ends up pregnant in an era when abortions were illegally performed in back street alleyways. Tough guy McQueen shows his softer side as he helps this virtual stranger solve her problem, while Wood blossoms as a nice Italian girl who learns to embrace her new *Sex and the Single Girl* lifestyle. (By the way, *Sex and the Single Girl* is another Natalie Wood flick well worth renting).

Mahogany (1975)—Singer Diana Ross, who is naturally as skinny as a model, stars as the title character—a young girl from the ghetto with a passion for street fashion who becomes a haute couture sensation. The impossibly handsome Billy Dee Williams is her main squeeze. Tony Perkins plays the psychotic photographer who becomes a little too possessive. Don't miss the rather notorious scene of dripping hot wax employed during sex play.

New Kind of Love, A (1963)—Department store clothing buyer Joanne Woodward heads to Paris to check out the new lines and falls in "hate" with real-life husband Paul Newman, playing a boorish newspaper man. The video box cover sums it up: "They love Paris. They hate each other. Can the City of Light become the City of Love?" Answer: yes. Don't miss *Green Acre*'s Eva Gabor, *Gigi*'s Maurice Chevalier, and a scene at Elizabeth Arden's Salon that will make you green with envy.

Object of My Affection, The (1998)—Attention fans of TV's *Friends* and *Will & Grace*, this motion picture is right up your alley. Jennifer Aniston stars as a pregnant single woman who elects to raise her child with her gay roommate, played by Paul Rudd (Phoebe's husband on *Friends*). If you like the film, you should read Stephen McCauley's terrific original novel.

Persuasion (1995)—In this lesser-known Jane Austen adaptation, good daughter Anne Elliot (Amanda Root) sacrifices a potential romance for the well-being of her thankless family and then is given a second chance when her secret love, Captain Wentworth (Ciaran Hinds), returns. Why isn't this wonderful BBC/A&E production more popular? Lack of movie star power (Ciaran Hinds is no Colin Firth).

Quick and the Dead, The (1995)—When Sharon Stone decides to do a Western, you know you're in for a lot of eye candy. Ms. Stone stars as a female gunslinger out to avenge her late father. Hunks in residence Leonardo DiCaprio and Russell Crowe add mightily to this flick's appeal.

Red Shoes, The (1948)—Not to be confused with the erotic series *Red Shoe Diaries*, this dance classic centers around a ballet performance featuring a pair of crimson slippers. The behind-the-scenes story line focuses on a ballerina (Moira Shearer) trying to keep her professional and personal life harmonious.

Something to Talk About (1995)—Written by *Thelma & Louise* scribe Callie Khouri, this family drama stars Julia Roberts as a happily married woman who discovers her husband Dennis Quaid (Meg Ryan's real-life ex) is cheating on her. The video box proclaims this is "a story about husbands, wives, parents, children, and other natural disasters." Kyra Sedgwick (Kevin Bacon's real-life wife) plays Julia's sister/best friend. Don't you agree that those two actresses really look like siblings?

That Touch of Mink (1962)—Surprisingly, Cary Grant takes on the Rock Hudson role in this 1962 Doris Day flick. Not surprisingly, Doris Day plays a virtuous career girl romanced by a flirtatious playboy (Grant). Millionaire Cary flies Doris to Bermuda on his private jet for a weekend of sin, but of course she doesn't succumb. Audrey Meadows shows up as Doris's best friend, while Gig Young subs for Tony Randall.

Unzipped (1995)—If the only documentary you own is *Madonna: Truth or Dare*, it's time to add another doc to your collection. Fashion designer Isaac Mizrahi allowed his then-boyfriend Douglas Keeve to document the behind-the-scenes madness leading up to a fashion runway show. In addition to great footage of supermodels being bitchy, you see what chick flicks inspire Isaac (Loretta Young's fur-lined classic, *The Call of the Wild*).

Valley of the Dolls (1967)—Back in the Sixties, publicity-hound author Jacqueline Susann wrote a trashy novel about three drug-addicted actresses that Hollywood quickly turned into a trashy flick starring Sharon Tate (Roman Polanski's wife, famously murdered by the Manson family), Patty Duke, and Barbara Parkins. Jacqueline Susann shows up on-screen as a reporter. Incidentally, the author's life story was made into a 2000 biopic, *Isn't She Great*, starring Bette Midler.

What's Up, Doc? (1972)—A screwball comedy à la *Bringing Up Baby*. Barbra Streisand plays a free spirit who decides bespectacled Ryan O'Neal is the cat's pajamas. Unfortunately, he's already engaged to stressed-out Madeline Kahn. There's a series of mix-ups involving matching plaid overnight cases and lots of physical comedy. Streisand and O'Neal followed up with a 1979 battle-of-the-sexes romantic comedy called *The Main Event*.

Xanadu (1980)—Back when roller skating was trendy, Hollywood decided to do a musical in which the main characters strap on skates. Fresh from her triumph in *Grease*, Olivia Newton-John wheels around in a

Farrah Fawcett hairstyle, acting as a muse to record cover painter Michael Beck (looking like a missing Bee Gee) and retired big band singer/hoofer Gene Kelly. What little plot there is centers around the two gents partnering up to open a nightclub called Xanadu. This unbelievably kitschy film is an amazing time capsule of terrible fashion choices.

Young Girls of Rochefort, The (1968)—Gene Kelly also makes an appearance in this French musical. Director Jacques Demy had such success with his 1964 Catherine Deneuve musical, *The Umbrellas of Cherbourg*, that he made another. Deneuve and her sister, Françoise Dorléac, play twins living in the seaside town of Rochefort. Although there are some lines of dialogue in this purposefully silly and candy-colored bon bon of a movie, the multiple love stories are conveyed in song and dance.

Zandalee (1991)—This New Orleans–based tale of sexual intrigue feels like it should be a Zalman King production (like *9½ Weeks*, *Wild Orchid*, *Two Moon Junction*, or *Red Shoe Diaries*). Erika Anderson, the sexually unsatisfied wife of Judge Reinhold, falls under the sway of her husband's bad-boy childhood friend Nicolas Cage. Fast forward through the dreary plot to get to the seduction scenes. Note: Nic Cage is oddly attractive with a mustache and a mullet. Who knew?

CHAPTER 11

Calendar Girl
Your Year of Chick Flicks

H ow essential do you consider chick flicks? Enough that you could watch one every single day? If a year of chick flicks is your idea of heaven, warm up your Blockbuster rental card, you're about to become a daily customer.

A Brand New You

January is the month to start anew. Your resolution: to gain inspiration from chick flick heroines who changed their lives for the better. You might not do something as radical as joining the army (as Goldie Hawn

1 *Working Girl* (1988)	**2** *The Mirror Has Two Faces* (1996)	**3** *Now, Voyager* (1942)	**4** **Viewer's choice:** *Sabrina* (1954) or *Sabrina* (1995)	
8 *She's All That* (1999)	**9** *Clueless* (1995)	**10** *Overboard* (1987)	**11** *Private Benjamin* (1980)	
15 *Miss Congeniality* (2000)	**16** *Love Potion #9* (1992)	**17** **Viewer's choice:** *Cinderella* (1950), *Cinderella* (1965), or *Cinderella* (1997)	**18** *Ever After* (1998)	
22 *Up Close & Personal* (1996)	**23** *Angie* (1994)	**24** *Evita* (1996)	**25** *Maid in Manhattan* (2002)	
29 *The Color Purple* (1985)	**30** *The World of Suzie Wong* (1960)	**31** **Viewer's choice:** *The Stepford Wives* (1975) or *The Stepford Wives* (2004)		

did in *Private Benjamin*), but you can certainly head to the gym, mall, hair salon, or spa to engineer your own glamorous makeover.

5 *The First Wives Club* (1996)	**6** *The Princess Diaries* (2001)	**7** *Moonstruck* (1987)
12 *G.I. Jane* (1997)	**13** *Swing Shift* (1984)	**14** *Coming Home* (1978)
19 Viewer's choice: *The Parent Trap* (1961) or *The Parent Trap* (1998)	**20** *My Fair Lady* (1964)	**21** Viewer's choice: *A Star Is Born* (1937), *A Star Is Born* (1954), or *A Star Is Born* (1976)
26 *Rachel, Rachel* (1968)	**27** *A New Kind of Love* (1963)	**28** *Georgy Girl* (1966)

JANUARY

Love Is in the Air

Celebrate Valentine's Day all month long with twenty-eight Cupid-approved love stories. Take note how the cinematic lovers "meet cute"—would such ploys work in real life?

1 Love Story (1970)	**2** Viewer's choice: *Love Affair* (1994), An *Affair to Remember* (1957), or *Love Affair* (1939)	**3** Love Serenade (1996)	**4** Love & Basketball (2000)	
8 Return to Me (2000)	**9** It Could Happen to You (1994)	**10** The Theory of Flight (1998)	**11** Murphy's Romance (1985)	
15 Truly Madly Deeply (1991)	**16** To Gillian on Her 37th Birthday (1996)	**17** A Walk in the Clouds (1995)	**18** The Bridges of Madison County (1995)	
22 Mad Love (1995)	**23** For Love of the Game (1999)	**24** When a Man Loves a Woman (1994)	**25** Barefoot in the Park (1967)	

5 Bed of Roses (1996)	**6** Mississippi Masala (1992)	**7** It Happened One Night (1934)
12 The Notebook (2004)	**13** Titanic (1997)	**14** Ghost (1990)
19 The American President (1995)	**20** Viewer's Choice: William Shakespeare's Romeo + Juliet (1996) or Romeo and Juliet (1968)	**21** Shakespeare in Love (1998)
26 Pillow Talk (1959)	**27** Lover Come Back (1961)	**28** Down with Love (2003)

FEBRUARY

Dance Fever

After watching these movies featuring fancy footwork, you'll want to strap on your dancing shoes.

1 Viewer's **Choice:** *Dirty Dancing* (1987) or *Dirty Dancing: Havana Nights* (2004)	**2** Viewer's **Choice:** *The Umbrellas of Cherbourg* (1964) or *The Young Girls of Rochefort* (1967)	**3** *Center Stage* (2000)	**4** *The Red Shoes* (1948)	
8 *Chicago* (2002)	**9** *Meet Me in St. Louis* (1944)	**10** *The Gay Divorcee* (1934)	**11** *Roberta* (1935)	
15 *Funny Face* (1957)	**16** *Silk Stockings* (1957)	**17** *Everyone Says I Love You* (1996)	**18** *Moulin Rouge* (2001)	
22 *Kiss Me Kate* (1953)	**23** *The King and I* (1956)	**24** Viewer's choice: *Annie* (1982) or *Annie* (1999)	**25** *The Rocky Horror Picture Show* (1975)	
29 *Staying Alive* (1983)	**30** Viewer's choice: *Grease* (1978) or *Grease 2* (1982)	**31** *Save the Last Dance* (2001)		

5 The Company (2003)	**6** The Turning Point (1977)	**7** Viewer's Choice: *Shall We Dance?* (1996) or *Shall We Dance?* (2004)
12 Top Hat (1935)	**13** Swing Time (1936)	**14** Daddy Long Legs (1955)
19 Strictly Ballroom (1992)	**20** Funny Lady (1975)	**21** Love's Labour's Lost (2000)
26 Sweet Charity (1969)	**27** Showgirls (1995)	**28** Coyote Ugly (2000)

MARCH

Costume Drama Extravaganza

Indulge in your love of period pieces. Let your e-mails pile up and your voice mail overflow as you lose yourself in stories about people who actually took the time to write letters.

1 *The Importance of Being Earnest* (2002)	**2** *An Ideal Husband* (1999)	**3** **Viewer's Choice:** *Emma* (1996) or *Jane Austen's Emma* (1997)	**4** **Viewer's Choice:** *Pride and Prejudice* (1940), *Pride and Prejudice* (1995), or *Pride and Prejudice* (2005)	
8 *Northanger Abbey* (1986)	**9** **Viewer's Choice:** *Wuthering Heights* (1939), *Wuthering Heights* (1970) or *Emily Brontë's Wuthering Heights* (1992)	**10** **Viewer's Choice:** *Jane Eyre* (1944) or *Jane Eyre* (1996)	**11** *Where Angels Fear to Tread* (1991)	
15 *Oscar and Lucinda* (1997)	**16** *The French Lieutenant's Woman* (1981)	**17** *Possession* (2002)	**18** *Gone with the Wind* (1939)	
22 *Anna and the King* (1999)	**23** *The Age of Innocence* (1993)	**24** *Hello, Dolly!* (1969)	**25** *The Portrait of a Lady* (1996)	
29 *First Knight* (1995)	**30** *Elizabeth* (1998)			

5 Sense and Sensibility (1995)	**6** Persuasion (1995)	**7** Mansfield Park (1999)
12 A Room with a View (1986)	**13** Lady Jane (1998)	**14** Howards End (1992)
19 Cold Mountain (2003)	**20** Jezebel (1938)	**21** Sommersby (1993)
26 Doctor Zhivago (1965)	**27** Cleopatra (1963)	**28** A Knight's Tale (2001)

A P R I L

Mother's Day Every Day

Mothers can be amazing heroes or stupendous villains. How does your own mom compare to these cinematic maternal powerhouses?

1 Hope Floats (1998)	**2** Riding in Cars with Boys (2001)	**3** Little Man Tate (1991)	**4** Viewer's choice: *Freaky Friday* (1976) or *Freaky Friday* (2003)	
8 White Oleander (2002)	**9** One True Thing (1998)	**10** Terms of Endearment (1983)	**11** The Horse Whisperer (1998)	
15 Alice Doesn't Live Here Anymore (1974)	**16** Viewer's choice: *Imitation of Life* (1934) or *Imitation of Life* (1959)	**17** Viewer's choice: *Stella Dallas* (1937) or *Stella* (1990)	**18** Viewer's choice: *Gypsy* (1962) or *Gypsy* (1993)	
22 Mermaids (1990)	**23** Mask (1985)	**24** Real Women Have Curves (2002)	**25** The Good Mother (1988)	
29 Pretty Baby (1978)	**30** The Buddy System (1984)	**31** Lorenzo's Oil (1992)		

	5 The Piano (1993)	**6** One Fine Day (1996)	**7** The Deep End of the Ocean (1999)
	12 Hideous Kinky (1999)	**13** The Hours (2002)	**14** Postcards from the Edge (1990)
	19 This Is My Life (1992)	**20** Mildred Pierce (1945)	**21** Mommie Dearest (1981)
	26 Shoot the Moon (1982)	**27** Stepmom (1998)	**28** Anywhere But Here (1999)

MAY

Say I Do

A couple can get married whenever they want, but there's something special about a June bride. Get the rice ready, you're going to be attending a lot of wedding ceremonies.

1 *How to Marry a Millionaire* (1953)	**2** *My Big Fat Greek Wedding* (2002)	**3** *Wedding Bell Blues* (1996)	**4** *Royal Wedding* (1951)	
8 *A Wedding* (1978)	**9** *The Best Man* (1999)	**10** *Honeymoon in Vegas* (1992)	**11** *Monsoon Wedding* (2001)	
15 *Steel Magnolias* (1989)	**16** **Viewer's choice:** *The Philadelphia Story* (1940) or *High Society* (1956)	**17** *Prelude to a Kiss* (1992)	**18** *Once Around* (1991)	
22 *Four Weddings and a Funeral* (1994)	**23** *The Wedding Planner* (2001)	**24** *The Wedding Singer* (1998)	**25** *Mrs. Winterbourne* (1996)	
29 *The Palm Beach Story* (1942)	**30** *I Was a Male War Bride* (1949)			

5 Betsy's Wedding (1990)	6 Muriel's Wedding (1994)	7 Viewer's choice: *Father of the Bride* (1950) or *Father of the Bride* (1991)
12 Bend It Like Beckham (2003)	13 My Best Friend's Wedding (1997)	14 Runaway Bride (1999)
19 Kissing Jessica Stein (2001)	20 True Love (1989)	21 28 Days (2000)
26 Feeling Minnesota (1996)	27 Soul Food (1997)	28 Gentlemen Prefer Blondes (1953)

JUNE

Foreign Adventure and Holiday Romance

Pack up the car for a road trip to the shore. Or grab your passport and visit the exotic locales you admire in the movies: Africa, Italy, France. If you can't do it in real life, here's your chance to vacation vicariously.

1 *Roman Holiday* (1953)	**2** *Chasing Liberty* (2004)	**3** *Summertime* (1955)	**4** *A Summer Place* (1959)	
8 *Paris—When It Sizzles* (1964)	**9** *Love in the Afternoon* (1957)	**10** *Two for the Road* (1967)	**11** *A Life Less Ordinary* (1997)	
15 *The Real Cancun* (2003)	**16** *Blue Crush* (2002)	**17** *How Stella Got Her Groove Back* (1998)	**18** *Summer Lovers* (1982)	
22 Viewer's choice: *Before Sunrise* (1995) or *Before Sunset* (2004)	**23** *Out of Africa* (1985)	**24** *I Dreamed of Africa* (2000)	**25** *Greystoke: The Legend of Tarzan, Lord of the Apes* (1984)	
29 *Only You* (1994)	**30** Viewer's choice: *The Roman Spring of Mrs. Stone* (1961) or *The Roman Spring of Mrs. Stone* (2003)	**31** *Paris Blues* (1961)		

	5 *The Greek Tycoon* (1978)	**6** *Forget Paris* (1995)	**7** *French Kiss* (1995)
	12 Come September (1961)	**13** *Forces of Nature* (1999)	**14** **Viewer's choice:** *Where the Boys Are* (1960) or *Where the Boys Are '84* (1984)
	19 **Viewer's choice:** *Blue Lagoon* (1980) or *Return to the Blue Lagoon* (1991)	**20** *Pauline at the Beach* (1983)	**21** *Bread and Tulips* (2000)
	26 *Three Coins in the Fountain* (1954)	**27** *Enchanted April* (1992)	**28** *Under the Tuscan Sun* (2003)

J U L Y

Getting Steamy

As any Neil Diamond fan will tell you, the eighth month is all about "Hot August Nights." These movies filled with naked hunks and steamy sex scenes certainly won't cool you down.

1 *Dangerous Beauty* (1998)	**2** *Belle de Jour* (1967)	**3** **Viewer's choice:** *9 ½ Weeks* (1986) or *Another 9 ½ Weeks* (1997) or *The First 9 ½ Weeks* (1998)	**4** **Viewer's choice:** *Wild Orchid* (1990) or *Wild Orchid II: Two Shades of Blue* (1992)	
8 *The Pillow Book* (1997)	**9** *Zandalee* (1991)	**10** *Original Sin* (2001)	**11** *sex, lies, and videotape* (1989)	
15 *Unfaithful* (2002)	**16** *Y Tu Mamá También* (2001)	**17** *Risky Business* (1983)	**18** *Henry & June* (1990)	
22 *Endless Love* (1981)	**23** *Eyes Wide Shut* (1999)	**24** **Viewer's choice:** *I am Curious (Yellow)* (1967) or *I am Curious (Blue)* (1968)	**25** *Betty Blue* (1986)	
29 *Like Water for Chocolate* (1993)	**30** *Looking for Mr. Goodbar* (1977)	**31** *American Gigolo* (1980)		

	5 **Viewer's choice:** *Two Moon Junction* (1988) or *Return to Two Moon Junction* (1994)	**6** *Delta of Venus* (1995)	**7** *Wide Sargasso Sea* (1993)
	12 *The Unbearable Lightness of Being* (1988)	**13** **Viewer's choice:** *The Postman Always Rings Twice* (1946) or *The Postman Always Rings Twice* (1981)	**14** *Body Heat* (1981)
	19 **Viewer's choice:** *Valmont* (1989) or *Dangerous Liaisons* (1988)	**20** *The Big Easy* (1987)	**21** *Swimming Pool* (2003)
	26 *The Story of O* (1975)	**27** *Crash* (1996)	**28** *Last Tango in Paris* (1973)

AUGUST

Back to School

Relive your school days via thirty cinema classics celebrating students and teachers. And the best part? You don't have to do any homework.

1 Girls Just Want to Have Fun (1985)	**2** The Night Before (1988)	**3** Lucas (1986)	**4** Say Anything (1989)
8 Pretty in Pink (1986)	**9** Sixteen Candles (1984)	**10** The Breakfast Club (1985)	**11** Some Kind of Wonderful (1987)
15 Mean Girls (2004)	**16** Heathers (1989)	**17** The Virgin Suicides (1999)	**18** crazy/ beautiful (2001)
22 Viewer's choice: The Trouble with Angels (1966) or Where Angels Go, Trouble Follows (1968)	**23** Reckless (1984)	**24** O (2001)	**25** Up the Down Staircase (1967)
29 Educating Rita (1983)	**30** Dangerous Minds (1995)		

	5 Bring It On (2000)	**6** Circle of Friends (1995)	**7** 10 Things I Hate About You (1999)
	12 Ferris Bueller's Day Off (1986)	**13** Can't Buy Me Love (1987)	**14** Sugar & Spice (2001)
	19 Pumpkin (2002)	**20** Cruel Intentions (1999)	**21** Sister Act 2: Back in the Habit (1993)
	26 Teacher's Pet (1958)	**27** The Prime of Miss Jean Brodie (1969)	**28** Mona Lisa Smile (2003)

SEPTEMBER

Be Afraid, Be Very Afraid

If you're wondering what to wear for Halloween, you'll find inspiration in these flicks about witches, vampires, ghosts, monsters, aliens, and demons.

1 Practical Magic (1998)	**2** Bell Book and Candle (1958)	**3** The Craft (1996)	**4** The Witches of Eastwick (1987)	
8 Hocus Pocus (1993)	**9** Bedknobs and Broomsticks (1971)	**10** Teen Witch (1989)	**11** The Others (2001)	
15 No Such Thing (2001)	**16** Vampire in Brooklyn (1995)	**17** Once Bitten (1985)	**18** Near Dark (1987)	
22 Queen of the Damned (2002)	**23** Bram Stoker's Dracula (1992)	**24** The Lost Boys (1987)	**25** The Hunger (1983)	
29 Firestarter (1984)	**30** The Seventh Sign (1988)	**31** Rosemary's Baby (1968)		

5 I Married a Witch (1942)	**6** Four Rooms (1995)	**7** The Crucible (1996)
12 The Company of Wolves (1985)	**13** Wolf (1994)	**14** Mary Shelley's Frankenstein (1994)
19 Nadja (1995)	**20** Buffy the Vampire Slayer (1992)	**21** Interview with the Vampire: The Vampire Chronicles (1994)
26 Starman (1984)	**27** Earth Girls Are Easy (1989)	**28** Carrie (1976)

OCTOBER

Family Ties

They may drive you crazy, especially on Turkey Day, but no one knows you better than your relatives. After watching these family relationship flicks, you'll be especially thankful for your own kin.

1 Hanging Up (2000)	**2** Marvin's Room (1996)	**3** *Hannah and Her Sisters (1986)*	**4** *Hilary and Jackie (1998)*
8 *Mystic Pizza (1988)*	**9** *Something to Talk About (1995)*	**10** *Slums of Beverly Hills (1998)*	**11** *The Accidental Tourist (1988)*
15 *Sweet Home Alabama (2002)*	**16** *The House of Yes (1997)*	**17** *The Fabulous Baker Boys (1989)*	**18** *In the Bedroom (2001)*
22 *Crossing Delancey (1988)*	**23** *The Snapper (1993)*	**24** *Mary Poppins (1964)*	**25** *Raising Helen (2004)*
29 Viewer's Choice: *Cheaper by the Dozen (2004)* or *Cheaper by the Dozen (1950)*	**30** *The Ice Storm (1997)*		

	5 Lovely & Amazing (2001)	**6** Gas Food Lodging (1992)	**7** The Other Sister (1999)
	12 Benny & Joon (1993)	**13** Corrina, Corrina (1994)	**14** Soapdish (1991)
	19 Moonlight Mile (2002)	**20** Seven Brides for Seven Brothers (1954)	**21** Viewer's Choice: The Lion in Winter (1968) or The Lion in Winter (2003)
	26 Pieces of April (2003)	**27** Home for the Holidays (1995)	**28** Life Is Sweet (1990)

NOVEMBER

'Tis the Season

Christmas is in the air and New Year's Eve is fast approaching. Make some eggnog and observe how others spend the holiday season.

1 For the Boys (1991)	**2** Viewer's choice: The Bishop's Wife (1947) or The Preacher's Wife (1996)	**3** Viewer's choice: Babes in Toyland (1961) or Babes in Toyland (1986)	**4** Viewer's choice: Christmas in Connecticut (1945) or Christmas in Connecticut (1992)	
8 Go (1999)	**9** Viewer's choice: Holiday Inn (1942) or White Christmas (1954)	**10** Falling in Love (1984)	**11** Serendipity (2001)	
15 8 Women (2002)	**16** Since You Went Away (1944)	**17** Kramer vs. Kramer (1979)	**18** Mrs. Santa Claus (1996)	
22 Mixed Nuts (1994)	**23** Viewer's choice: Little Women (1933), Little Women (1949), or Little Women (1994)	**24** Viewer's choice: Auntie Mame (1958) or Mame (1974)	**25** Viewer's choice: Miracle on 34th Street (1947) or Miracle on 34th Street (1994)	
29 Penny Serenade (1941)	**30** Bachelor Mother (1939)	**31** When Harry Met Sally... (1989)		

	5 *Bridget Jones's Diary* (2001)	**6** *Love Actually* (2003)	**7** *Nutcracker: The Motion Picture* (1986)
	12 *Sleepless in Seattle* (1993)	**13** *Untamed Heart* (1993)	**14** *While You Were Sleeping* (1995)
	19 *Prancer* (1989)	**20** *The Homecoming: A Christmas Story* (1971)	**21** *Yours, Mine and Ours* (1968)
	26 *Hav Plenty* (1997)	**27** *Someone Like You* (2001)	**28** *Peter's Friends* (1992)

DECEMBER

CHAPTER 12

Mattress Dancing

The Sexiest Scenes Ever Captured on Celluloid

Have you ever noticed that sexual encounters in chick flicks appear so much more glamorous than real-world mating? Scripted situations, body doubles, professional lighting, carefully placed cameras, and a lush soundtrack ensure that doing the nasty on screen looks pretty darn scrumptious. The following ten steamy encounters are Hollywood magic-making at its best.

10. Leonard Whiting climbs Olivia Hussey's balcony in **Romeo and Juliet** (1968)

Didn't reading *Romeo and Juliet* seem boring back when you were in high school? After viewing Franco Zeffirelli's film, you'll never think of the balcony scene the same way again. There's young Leonard Whiting, all sweaty and passionate, leaping up the tree to reach Olivia Hussey. And what about the post–wedding night scene, in which the two lovers are reluctant to admit dawn has arrived. Beginning with a shot of Whiting's bare butt and culminating in his hasty dressing as the household begins to stir, this sexy sheet-rustling encounter isn't your high school English class's version of Shakespeare. Three decades after Zeffirelli's revolutionary adaptation, director Baz Luhrmann brought a different brand of youthful sexiness to Shakespeare's star-crossed lovers, creating a modernized, Americanized version starring Leonardo DiCaprio and Claire Danes. In Luhrmann's highly stylized take, the balcony scene is now played in a swimming pool, with the two teens treading water as they declare their love. The morning-after bedroom session (which, by the way, was the very first scene the director shot during production) doesn't reach Zeffirelli heights, but it still has an irresistible youthful zest.

9. George Clooney and Jennifer Lopez take a break from playing cops and robbers in *Out of Sight* (1998)

How's this for meeting cute? When convicted bank robber George Clooney makes a jailbreak, federal marshall Jennifer Lopez is waiting in the prison's parking lot with a loaded rifle. With the help of his getaway driver Ving Rhames, George quickly disarms her, shoves her in the car trunk, and climbs in after her. Close quarters result in friendly groping and seductive banter. Consequently, when they're freed from the trunk, George is reluctant to let J.Lo go. Later, after they go their separate ways, Jen fantasizes about finding the outlaw's hideout, capturing George as he lounges in the bath, and then climbing in the tub to join him. When they finally do reunite in a hotel bar hours before Clooney is scheduled to commit another felony, director Steven Soderbergh increases the sexual tension by playing with time, intercutting the would-be lover's seductive wordplay in the hotel bar with images of the two disrobing later in their hotel room. A night with bad boy George makes good girl Jennifer wish they weren't on opposite sides of the law.

8. Paraplegic Jon Voight shows Jane Fonda what she's been missing in Coming Home (1978)

In *Coming Home*, Jane Fonda is the wife of brutish career army officer Bruce Dern. Their marital bed consists of missionary position sex, during which she doesn't move a muscle. Is it any wonder Fonda's ripe for an affair with angry paraplegic veteran Jon Voight? Although Voight doesn't have use of his legs, he compensates in ways that make Jane a very happy adulteress. Their four-minute graphic sexual encounter culminates in the soldier's wife's first orgasm.

7. Diane Lane discovers adultery in the afternoon with a book-loving Frenchman is more appealing than marital relations with Richard Gere in Unfaithful (2002)

If you were married to Richard Gere, would you be tempted to cheat? In this flick, suburban wife and mother Diane Lane finds herself unable to resist the lure of handsome Olivier Martinez. The highlight of the film is Lane's delayed hysterical reaction on the train ride back home when she flashes back to her seduction scene in Martinez's book-lined apartment. The bathtub scene with Gere is pretty hot, too.

6. Daniel Day-Lewis romps with Lena Olin before and after he marries Juliette Binoche in The Unbearable Lightness of Being (1988)

Take off your clothes. That's doctor Daniel Day-Lewis's standard pickup line. And because he is a sexy beast, women eagerly shed their garments to tussle with the studly brain surgeon. The line even works with shy Juliette Binoche, who arrives on Daniel's doorstep uninvited. Although Day-Lewis tells lover Lena Olin that he doesn't let women stay overnight at his place, the good doctor finds himself living with and ultimately marrying Juliette. However, a sex addict cannot be tamed, and Daniel continues to have carnal relations with Lena Olin (and other women). In a movie chockful of bedroom romps, Olin's initial athletic enjoyment of her physician lover is certainly a highlight. Bonus points for creative use of mirrors and a bowler hat.

5. Clark Gable carries Vivien Leigh up the stairs in **Gone with the Wind** (1939)

Clark Gable's marriage proposal to Vivien Leigh is accompanied by a smoldering kiss and the assurance that none of her previous husbands could pleasure her like he will. Judging from what we see of their New Orleans honeymoon, Vivien seems pleased with their arrangement. What doesn't please her is her expanding waistline post-childbirth. Banishing Clark from further baby-making activities, Vivien continues her love-from-afar obsession with her best friend's husband. Clark can only take so much, and after a drunken late-night confrontation with his wife, he hauls Vivien up their gaudy mansion's grand staircase. We aren't witness to what happens next, but Vivien's extremely happy behavior the morning after indicates it was an earth-shattering encounter.

4. Mickey Rourke feeds Kim Basinger in front of the fridge in **9 1/2 Weeks** (1986)

Who would have thought the common household refrigerator could be packed with so many objects to aid in sensual pleasure? In *9 1/2 Weeks*, dominating businessman Mickey Rourke tells his current mistress, art gallery–worker Kim Basinger, to close her eyes and leads her to the kitchen. Always pushing Kim to explore new sensual boundaries during their highly erotic encounters, Mickey feeds her a series of treats: black olives, strawberries, jalapeños, honey, and milk. Sounds like a recipe for an upset stomach, but it looks very sexy on screen.

3. Susan Sarandon and Kevin Costner twist the night away in **Bull Durham** (1988)

While baseball fan Susan Sarandon spends most of *Bull Durham* dating rookie pitcher Tim Robbins, in the end she wises up and spends a night with seasoned catcher Kevin Costner. After a bout of mattress dancing, Kevin and Susan refuel with a bowl of cereal, followed by sex on the kitchen table. Next on the night's agenda is a robe-clad sock hop in the living room, capped by a sensuous candle-lit bath for two. Somewhere in the night he also paints her toenails. Taking his leave in the morning, Kev jots a thoughtful note and leaves an apple on his still-slumbering lover's pillow to sweeten the farewell. Too good to be true!

2. Dennis Quaid turns Ellen Barkin's bad luck around in **The Big Easy** (1987)

Bad boy New Orleans cop Dennis Quaid knows good girl district attorney Ellen Barkin thinks he's corrupt. And he is corrupt. But he's also a good detective who wants to see right prevail. So he helps Ms. Barkin with her investigations, even showing up at her office with a pizza box hiding crucial documents. How can Ellen resist Dennis's Cajun accent and killer smile? Their lovemaking scene, in which Barkin protests that she's never had much luck with sex and Quaid responds that her luck is about to change, is interrupted by a call to return to duty. Still, Dennis gives Ellen such pleasure that we're not surprised when the movie ends with the newly wedded couple blissfully dancing around their apartment.

1. Geena Davis lets Brad Pitt into her motel room in **Thelma & Louise** (1991)

Here's a helpful tip: Think twice before having hot sex in a hotel room with a complete stranger. Sounds a little seedy, doesn't it? It sounds even worse if the guy's a hitchhiker you just picked up on the highway, right? But if he looks like Brad Pitt, you might be tempted to reconsider. Especially if you're Geena Davis, married to a lamebrained lug who tries to control your every move. A wild card like Brad looks mighty tempting, showing off those six-pack abs while he demonstrates how armed robbery can be a pleasant experience for everyone involved. No wonder Geena has a huge grin on her face when she shows up the next morning for breakfast with Susan Sarandon. However, Geena's roll in the hay doesn't come cheap. Here's another tip: if you're going to let a stranger in your room, don't leave thousands of dollars lying around on the nightstand. It's just too much temptation. (However, if you have the money to spare, like Richard Gere's corporate raider does in *Pretty Woman*, the upfront payment of a few grand for seven nights spent in a five-star hotel with a babe like Julia Roberts doesn't seem like that bad a deal.) Last tip: Remember the added benefit of doing the wild thing in a rented room— if you make a mess, you aren't the one who has to clean up afterward.

CHAPTER 13

Pretty in Prada
Cinema's Most Memorable Fashion Statements

H ave you ever noticed how guys love to repeat lines from movies?
I have a friend who can quote almost every line from *Caddyshack*.
Why anyone would ever want to spend time memorizing lines of
dialogue in order to quote them at will, I'll never know. With rare exception, chick flicks aren't treasured for their bon mots. What they offer is
something more worthy of our attention: glamour. Don't you often sit
in a movie theater, coveting the lifestyle you see represented on screen?
The Wedding Planner director Adam Shankman knows all about the
power of silver screen glitz. He recalls "the old-fashioned glamour of
some of my favorite films, like *His Girl Friday*, *Bringing Up Baby*, and
Roman Holiday. These films were populated with truly beautiful people
who bantered with smart dialogue, wore beautiful clothes, and lived in
beautiful settings. For the audience, it was pure entertainment. It lifted
you out of your seat a little bit, out of your life a little bit. It became another world."

How do directors of chick flicks achieve such a state of glamour? They hire experts. A score of writers think up those fabulous situations, production designers construct those exquisite settings, and extremely attractive movie stars populate those locations with their magnificent faces and figures. And the reason those actors always dress better than ordinary people do is because they have an entire wardrobe department devoted to assembling their look.

Costume designers put a great deal of thought into how characters express themselves via their clothing. Take Pamela Withers, who worked with director Adam Shankman to bring Jennifer Lopez and Matthew McConaughey's Mary and Steve to life in *The Wedding Planner*. "Adam and I saw Mary's style as very sophisticated, conservative and timeless, like such everlasting icons as Audrey Hepburn, Grace Kelly, or Jacqueline Kennedy. Mary also seemed like a woman who saved her money and invested it in a few good designer pieces. I dressed her in such things as a classic blue Armani cotton sheath, a tan leather Prada coat, and an Emporio Armani two-piece top and skirt with a little cardigan. The audience may not be used to seeing Jennifer Lopez like this, but she looks stunning. Mary starts out dressing very businesslike when the film begins, but her wardrobe becomes a touch sexier, lighter, and romantic as the film goes on. In the scene where Mary and Steve meet and he rescues her, she's in bright blue and tan, and he's in navy and chocolate, so they complement each other. Conversely, when they're dancing the tango together, I put Mary in a red dress to symbolize anger and passion, and Steve wears a maroon shirt, which clashes just a little with her dress. Subconsciously, it jars you just a touch and shows the disconnectedness at that time in their relationship."

Let's celebrate the work of these highly dedicated designers and list the most memorable fashion statements ever to come out of a Hollywood wardrobe department.

Most Memorable Pretty in Pink Ensemble: Marilyn Monroe's strapless number in Gentlemen Prefer Blondes (1953)

Sure, you'd think Molly Ringwald would easily win this category based on her starring role in the movie of the same name, but her *Pretty in Pink* prom dress hasn't aged well. It's too Eighties, and not in a good way (although, thankfully, the actual movie is too Eighties in the right way). Another honorable mention is the *Legally Blonde 2: Red, White & Blonde* postmodern tribute to Jacqueline Kennedy's famous pink pillbox hat and matching boxy suit worn by Reese Witherspoon when she hits the nation's capital. However, the pink dress that still sets feminine hearts aflutter half a century after it made its cinematic debut is Marilyn Monroe's "Diamonds Are a Girl's Best Friend" stage costume in *Gentlemen Prefer Blondes*. This gown is so iconic that even Madonna covets it. Remember the knockoff in the "Material Girl" music video?

Most Memorable Little Black Dress: Demi Moore's $5K frock in Indecent Proposal (1993)

An essential item in every woman's wardrobe, the little black dress is a staple item in movies, too. Just look at the *Sweet Home Alabama* DVD cover—what's Reese Witherspoon wearing? You guessed it. Of course, nobody knows how versatile black can be better than Audrey Hepburn, who spends practically all of *Breakfast at Tiffany's* wearing variations on the same theme. However, the actress who wears a frock noir that caused a nationwide copycat craze is Demi Moore. While no reasonable woman wanted to emulate Ms. Moore's head-shaving in *G.I. Jane*, we all wanted the multi-strapped glad rag she wears while Robert Redford propositions her in *Indecent Proposal*. Well worth the five grand Redford pays for it.

Most Memorable Ball Gown:
Cinderella's homemade creation in
Cinderella
(1950)

Say you're going out for a very glamorous night on the town with a multimillionaire or a U.S. senator and your closet isn't exactly bursting at the seams with fancy gowns. What do you do? Julia Roberts and Jennifer Lopez face this quandary in *Pretty Woman* and *Maid in Manhattan*, respectively. In their specific cases, these women don't have a dime to their names but they do have a secret weapon: they live/work in very expensive hotels with ritzy dress shops located in the lobby. Gowns are quickly borrowed for the evening. Julia looks stunning in a lacy number, while Jennifer shines in a floor-length piece. However, the poor working girl who best transforms herself into the belle of the ball is Cinderella. In the animated Disney movie, Cinderella's fairy godmother works a little Bibbidi-Bobbidi-Boo magic, and the mice and birds whip up a frothy gown so stunning it captivates a prince. Now that's magic.

Most Memorable Bridesmaid Dress: Charlotte Coleman's disaster in Four Weddings and a Funeral (1994)

Brides, if you're trying to get ideas for your attendants' dresses, garner inspiration from the many weddings that take place in chick flicks. The bridesmaid's dress that will make you shudder in horror is the unforgettable frock Charlotte Coleman wears for the second ceremony in *Four Weddings and a Funeral*. As they did in the film's first wedding sequence, Hugh Grant and his redheaded roommate Charlotte oversleep and have to make a mad dash to get to the church on time. Picture Charlotte, hiking up her masses of underskirts so she can better sprint down the London streets. When the gown's elaborate bow falls to the pavement, she ignores it, hoping no one will notice it's missing. Wrong! Ms. Coleman marches down the aisle with the backside of her dress gaping wide open, blue underpants clearly exposed for all to see. How embarrassing for everyone involved.

Most Memorable Costume Party Outfit: Rabbit ears and bunny tails, worn by both Renée Zellweger in Bridget Jones's Diary (2001) and Reese Witherspoon in Legally Blonde (2001)

What does a chick wear to a costume party? In *Mermaids*, Cher concocts an elaborate deep sea diva costume, complete with tail. Barbra Streisand dresses like Harpo Marx in *The Way We Were*, while the cast of Woody Allen's *Everyone Says I Love You* puts on Groucho glasses for a Marx Brothers–themed New Year's Eve party at the Ritz. Do you remember the costume worn by both Renée Zellweger in *Bridget Jones's Diary* and Reese Witherspoon in *Legally Blonde*? The blonde bombshells stand out like sore thumbs—because the gatherings they attend in their sexy bunny outfits turn out not to be costume parties after all.

Most Memorable Outer Space Gear: Jane Fonda's molded plastic chestplate and go-go boots in Barbarella (1968)

In the real world, we're not yet living on Mars, but in movies women have already established a beachhead in outer space. While Princess Leia's extremely unflattering cinnamon-bun hairdo and shapeless white smock in *Star Wars* make us fear for our sartorial choices in outer space, we have one shining example to give us hope: *Barbarella*. During her many adventures seeking the missing scientist Durand Durand, Jane Fonda changes into one pure Sixties sex kitten fantasy ensemble after another. If this is what the future is going to bring, prep by stocking up on go-go boots.

Most Memorable Shirt: Jennifer Beals's ripped sweatshirt in **Flashdance** (1983)

Want to suggestively remove your bra in the presence of a prospective lover? Watch how Jennifer Beals does it in *Flashdance*. Her collarless baggy sweatshirt allows easy removal of restraining undergarments. No wonder the ripped collar became such a popular style in the Eighties. Why her leg warmers also became popular remains a mystery.

Most Memorable Hat: Richard Gere's officer's cap in **An Officer and a Gentleman** (1982)

Back when women wore hats every day, a plethora of chapeaux paraded across the silver screen. While Lena Olin's bowler gets a workout in *The Unbearable Lightness of Being*, very few modern hats have real importance. Except for one, which has such power it's the last image of the film. In *An Officer and a Gentleman*, naval officer candidate Richard Gere is warned to stay away from the local girls, who are notorious for trying to marry a navy man as a way out of their depressed town. Richard nevertheless hooks up with paper mill worker Debra Winger. Midway through the movie, Debra tries on Richard's uniform cap while they tussle in a motel room, but that's a throwaway moment. The moment that counts is when Gere, in full dress whites, shows up at the factory to spirit Winger away while her mother, best friend, and fellow female co-workers cheer. The very last image of the film is Debra removing her officer's cap and putting it on her own head. Job well done!

Most Memorable Jacket: Madonna's glitzy sheath in **Desperately Seeking Susan** (1985)

The easiest way to assemble an outfit similar to what you see on the big screen is to follow in the footsteps of the originators: Scour the second-hand clothing stores for unique pieces. "We practically devoured thrift stores that had all kinds of fabulous designer clothing," reports *How to Lose a Guy in 10 Days* costume designer Karen Patch. Characters in chick flicks also score treasures in vintage shops—remember Rosanna Arquette buying Madonna's pyramid jacket in *Desperately Seeking Susan*? In the movie, Rosanna plays a frustrated housewife fixated on a series of personal ads addressing someone named Susan. Curious, she goes to one of the ad's stated rendezvous spots and spots Susan: a funky troublemaker played by Madonna. When the Material Girl trades the jacket off her back for a pair of boots in a thrift store, Ms. Arquette quickly snaps up the discarded garment, which she wears for the rest of the movie. If eBay had existed back then, that jacket would have sold for a fortune.

Most Memorable Sleepwear:
Barbra Streisand's nightie in
On a Clear Day You Can See Forever
(1970)

When it comes to suitable sleepwear, many chick flick heroines wear men's shirts. Jane Fonda looks adorable wearing Robert Redford's pajama top in *Barefoot in the Park*, Annette Bening dons Michael Douglas's white dress shirt in *The American President*, and Ellen Barkin slips into Dennis Quaid's police uniform top in *The Big Easy*. Of course, fancy nightgowns, peignoirs, and lingerie are also timeless options worn by countless chick flick characters. You can pretty much duplicate any look you've seen on the big screen with a trip to Victoria's Secret. Achieving the absolute ultimate in sleepwear, however, will take a little more effort. The most impressive nightwear ever portrayed in a chick flick has to be the ensemble worn by Barbra Streisand in the musical *On a Clear Day You Can See Forever*. In a movie swimming in smashing fashion statements (both contemporary and period), the real eye-opener is Babs's flowered nightie. The wallflower's nightgown matches her floral sheets and bedroom wallpaper! Now that's the sign of a costume designer putting some major thought into what a character wears.

CHAPTER 14

Pass the Kleenex

Definitive Tearjerking
Portraits of Love and Death

While romantic comedies are wonderful, sometimes chick flick enthusiasts want nothing more than a good excuse to cry. That's why we can never have enough tearjerkers. Nothing tugs on the tear ducts harder than death scenes. Actors love to play them, and we love to watch them with hankies in hand. Death may not be proud, but it's always heartbreaking. Let us count the ways.

Dying daughter: Steel Magnolias (1989) and Terms of Endearment (1983)

Who can watch the hospital scenes in these two classic tearjerkers and remain dry-eyed? In both films, the steel-willed mamas (Sally Field and Shirley MacLaine, respectively) are vocal in their displeasure regarding their daughters' life choices, but no one fights harder to try to keep death at bay. And in both cases, the daughters' terminal illnesses (diabetes for Julia Roberts, cancer for Debra Winger) are even more tragic because they leave behind children that their aging mothers will now have to raise. By the way, there actually is a sequel for *Terms of Endearment* entitled *The Evening Star* (1996). Rest assured, MacLaine and Winger's kids are doing fine.

Dying mother: One True Thing (1998)

Based on Anna Quindlen's novel of the same name, this movie benefits from the casting of the incomparable Meryl Streep as the Martha Stewart–like perfect mother of writer Renée Zellweger. I defy anyone who has lost their mother not to shed copious tears as Ms. Streep's health declines despite Renée's best efforts.

Dying girlfriend: A Walk to Remember (2002)

Isn't cinematic young love so much more interesting when it's tragic? Based on the popular novel by Nicholas Sparks, this teen melodrama features Shane West as a mixed-up bad boy and Mandy Moore as the Christian girl who reforms him. Young Shane West does a pretty good summing up of this tearjerker by reporting that "the movie starts out with a scene that reminds you of *The Outsiders*, then develops into a love story, and then takes a whole different tone." If you haven't guessed it by now, Miss Moore doesn't make it through to the end credits.

Dying wife: Love Story (1970)

The movie begins with Ryan O'Neal wondering what one can say about a dying girl who loves the Beatles, Bach, and him. Lots, apparently. The story flashes back to follow the romance between rich Harvard man O'Neal and poor Radcliffe student Ali MacGraw. Ms. MacGraw's youthful beauty remains untarnished even in the last stages of life.

Dying husband: Ghost (1990)

Yes, there is that infamous scene where Patrick Swayze and Demi Moore make a pottery wheel seem like the most erotic device ever known to mankind. But what gets the waterworks going is Demi's on-screen reaction to husband Swayze's murder. Fans of love stories featuring recently departed spouses who refuse to give up the ghost should check out the British flick *Truly Madly Deeply* which was made a year later and has a similar haunting story line.

Dying best friend (female): Beaches (1988)

Like the mother-daughter teams in *Steel Magnolias* and *Terms of Endearment*, childhood friends Bette Midler and Barbara Hershey spend most of the movie disapproving of each other's life choices, but rally at the end when one of them starts knocking on death's door. For those of you who haven't seen *Beaches* yet, I won't ruin it for you by telling you which friend crosses over, but in the tried-and-true tearjerking formula, the remaining woman is left to raise the dead woman's child.

Dying best friend (male): My Girl (1991)

Preteen Anna Chlumsky has spent her whole life surrounded by the grim reaper: Her mother's dead and her father is a mortician. So when her bespectacled best friend Macaulay Culkin gets a fatal bee sting, we shouldn't be caught unaware, but we are. In case you're wondering, the sequel, *My Girl 2* (1994), is much more cheerful.

Dying boss: Dying Young (1991)

Don't worry, Julia Roberts is not the one dying this time. The robustly healthy Ms. Roberts is the paid companion to Campbell Scott, a rich loner fighting leukemia. It may sound grim, but the plot becomes romantic and heartwarming as Campbell decides Julia's loving arms are more healing than another round of chemotherapy. Look for Campbell Scott's real-life mother, Colleen Dewhurst, playing the neighboring winery woman. Trivia fans please note: Julia's *Steel Magnolia*'s mom, Sally Field, produced this film.

And More . . .

If you've got more tears to shed, here are fifteen additional movies with varying tragic plot elements you might enjoy:

- *An Affair to Remember* (1957)—You saw in *Sleepless in Seattle* how Meg Ryan, Rosie O'Donnell, and Rita Wilson all boo-hoo'd over this flick. You'll do the same as recently crippled Deborah Kerr fights so hard not to reveal her physical weakness to Cary Grant.

- *The Boy in the Plastic Bubble* (1976)—John Travolta plays a young man whose extreme immune deficiencies force him to live in a germ-free environment. When he falls in love with neighborhood beauty Glynnis O'Connor, life in a plastic bubble loses its appeal. Look for Robert Reed, the dad from *The Brady Bunch*, as Travolta's pop.

- *The Bridges of Madison County* (1995)—Who would have thought that tough guy director Clint Eastwood would make a movie that's even more melodramatic than Robert James Waller's novel? Dirty Harry and Meryl Streep play a couple of strangers who share a magical few days while housewife Meryl's family is away. You'll cry because of the hard choices both must make once their interlude comes to an end.

- *The Color Purple* (1985)—Based on Alice Walker's novel, this epic story of hardship among African Americans launched the careers of Whoopi Goldberg and Oprah Winfrey. Steven Spielberg directed, and we all know that man knows how to wring tears from a stone.

- *Here on Earth* (2000)—In this portrait of small town teen romance, one of the teenagers's health takes a turn for the worse. Is it sweethearts Leelee Sobieski and Josh Hartnett, or rich kid Chris Klein?

- *I Am Sam* (2001)—Mentally challenged Sean Penn is doing his best to raise precocious daughter Dakota Fanning, but not everyone believes he's up to the challenge. Hotshot legal eagle Michelle Pfeiffer has to win the custody hearing if we want a happy ending.

- *The Joy Luck Club* (1993)—Yes, great tearjerker novels tend to make great tearjerker movies. Fans of Amy Tan's book know what terrible decisions a mother in a war-torn country could be forced to make.

- *The Little Princess* (1939)—Privileged boarding school student Shirley Temple finds herself in dire straits when her beloved soldier father is declared dead. The 1995 remake with Liesel Matthews is also worth a view.

- *Marvin's Room* (1996)—People of all ages are ill and dying in this drama. Diane Keaton and Meryl Streep portray estranged sisters of opposite temperaments. Leonardo DiCaprio brings a youth factor as Meryl's son who prefers his aunt Diane.

- *My Life Without Me* (2003)—Young wife and mother Sarah Polley has only a few months to live. Composing a daring list of things to do before she dies (including finding her children a new mother), Polley checks them off one by one.

- *The Outsiders* (1983)—This hunkfest melodrama about friendship, family, sacrifice, and tragedy among a makeshift group of juvenile delinquents is based on a perennial teen cult novel, written by a teenage girl (so you know it's going to be great).

- *A Patch of Blue* (1965)—Blonde Elizabeth Hartman plays a sheltered blind woman who adores Sidney Poitier and doesn't understand why her mother and others oppose their relationship.

- *Sophie's Choice* (1982)—It's Meryl Streep's turn to make a difficult wartime decision about the fate of her two children.

- *Stella Dallas* (1937)—The film's original theatrical release posters read "Ridiculed for her clothes, her cheapness, her vulgarity, she shows the world what true mother-love means." Barbara Stanwyck stars as a hopelessly lower-class matriarch who sacrifices her own happiness to ensure daughter Anne Shirley will live happily with her wealthy father. The movie was remade in 1990 as *Stella*, starring Bette Midler in the Stanwyck role.

- *Untamed Heart* (1993)—Christian Slater knows he has a heart condition but nevertheless falls for spunky waitress Marisa Tomei. Can his ticker make it to the end credits? Watch and see.

CHAPTER 15

Do Gentlemen Really Prefer Blondes

Essential Chick Flick Discussion Points

S
ure, some chick flicks are disposable mindless entertainment, but many stick with you long after you've hit the rewind button. Ever find yourself pondering what you would do if you were in the character's shoes? Perhaps you like to contemplate how events that take place on the silver screen apply to the real world. These absolutely essential discussion points will spur further thought.

• In *My Best Friend's Wedding*, Cameron Diaz gets hitched to Julia's guy while Ms. Roberts is left to dance at their wedding with her gay friend Rupert Everett. If you were Julia, would you consider this to be a satisfactory ending?

• Meg Ryan and Tom Hanks are very believable as an on-screen couple in *Sleepless in Seattle* and *You've Got Mail*, but in real life Tom is married to actress Rita Wilson (who has a cameo in *Sleepless in Seattle* as his good friend). Why is it that in real life men who seem so perfect for you always seem to be married to other women?

• In the film *Two Weeks Notice*, Sandra Bullock resists at first but then ends up becoming romantically involved with boss Hugh Grant. What are the pros and cons of dating your employer?

• In *Four Weddings and a Funeral*, many of the characters meet their potential mates at the titular gatherings. In your experience, which is the better venue for trolling for dates, a wedding or a funeral?

• In *Moonstruck*, Nicolas Cage's ultimate dream date is taking Cher to the opera. What is your ultimate dream date?

• If your boyfriend were to stand outside your window and blast a love song to win your affections like John Cusack does in *Say Anything*, which song would you like to hear?

• Kevin Costner has played a golfer in *Tin Cup* and a baseball player in *Bull Durham*, *For Love of the Game*, and *Field of Dreams*. In general, which jocks do you find sexier: basketball players, football players, baseball players, hockey players, or golfers?

• If he wants to be this generation's Cary Grant, George Clooney needs to do more chick flicks. Which Cary Grant movie do you think should be remade as a Clooney vehicle?

• In *The Princess Bride*, Robin Wright's character Buttercup is reported to be one of the most beautiful women in the world. Who in your opinion are the three most beautiful women alive today?

• In *The American President*, Michael Douglas certainly makes a sexy prez. If asked to name the top three sexiest commanders in chief (either in films or in real life), who would you put on the list?

• In *Flashdance*, after a hard day welding, Jennifer Beals struts her stuff on stage in the local club. Under what circumstances would you consider exotic dancing a suitable second job?

• In *Grease*, both John Travolta and Olivia Newton-John have their own cliques. If you had to assemble your own Pink Ladies entourage, whom would you initiate into the group? Would the pink jacket be optional or mandatory?

• In *Gentlemen Prefer Blondes*, both the blonde and the brunette end up snagging a man. In your experience, is it true that men prefer women with lighter locks?

• In *Somewhere in Time*, Christopher Reeve travels in time to meet an actress he's obsessed with. If you could do the same, which actor from the past would you go back to romance?

• In *Titanic*, Kate Winslet is safe in a lifeboat when she throws herself back onto the sinking *Titanic* to find Leonardo DiCaprio. For whom would you make a similar sacrifice?

• In *Casablanca*, Ingrid Bergman gets on the plane, leaving Humphrey Bogart on the tarmac. In *When Harry Met Sally . . .* , Billy Crystal and Meg Ryan have differing opinions on what *Casablanca*'s ending means. Do you think Ingrid did the right thing?

• In *Freaky Friday*, mother and daughter swap bodies for a day. If you could be someone else for a Friday, who would be your dream switch? Your nightmare?

• In *Steel Magnolias*, Sally Field gives up her kidney for daughter Julia Roberts. Under what circumstances would you be willing to donate an organ?

- In *Never Been Kissed*, Drew Barrymore enjoys a flirtation with her high school English teacher. Did you ever have a crush on a teacher?

- In *Bridget Jones's Diary*, Renée Zellweger can't resist Hugh Grant, even though she knows he's a cad. Why do we always like the bad boys?

- Shakespeare's *The Taming of the Shrew* was Americanized, modernized, and high schoolized to become *10 Things I Hate About You*. If you were to make such a list about your sweetie, what would be on your roster of pet peeves?

- In *Moulin Rouge*, Ewan McGregor sings a medley of love songs to woo Nicole Kidman. How would you react if serenaded in real life?

- In *Pillow Talk*, Doris Day's love interest is Rock Hudson. Back in the day, audiences had no idea that the actor was gay. How many of your girlfriends are dating or are married to men whom you think are secretly gay?

- In *Working Girl*, secretary Melanie Griffith has to lose her Staten Island hairdo in order to pass as a sophisticated executive. When it comes to hairstyles suitable for the workplace, is less more and how high is too high?

- In films like *Chocolat* and *Like Water for Chocolate*, confectionery is used as a metaphor for passion. Under what circumstances is chocolate better than sex?

- *Ever After* is a girl power retelling of the *Cinderella* story. What other fairy tales need to be updated to the twenty-first century way of thinking?

- In *Something's Gotta Give*, Diane Keaton has two fellows competing for her attention. In your opinion, under what circumstances is it acceptable to date (a) your daughter's boyfriend and (b) your boyfriend's doctor? Which is less horrifying, and why?

• In *Bull Durham*, Susan Sarandon spends the first half of the movie with Tim Robbins and the last half with Kevin Costner. What are the pros and cons of dating a rookie versus a pro?

• In *City of Angels*, Meg Ryan is romanced by a celestial being. In *Michael*, Andie MacDowell is attracted to John Travolta's winged persona. Do you believe there are angels among us, and are they suitable date material?

• In *The Ghost and Mrs. Muir* and *The Others*, houses are haunted by unfriendly spirits. Have you ever had a poltergeist experience?

• In *On a Clear Day You Can See Forever*, Barbra Streisand is revealed to have lived several past lives. Do you believe in reincarnation?

• Goldie Hawn joins the army to get a brand-new life in *Private Benjamin*. In *Hideous Kinky*, Kate Winslet packs up her daughters and heads to Morocco. What extreme action would you take if you wanted to radically change your life?

• In *Miss Congeniality*, gangly FBI agent Sandra Bullock is transformed into a beauty queen. If you were forced to compete in a beauty pageant tomorrow, which do you think would be your strongest category: swimsuit, evening gown, poise, or talent?

• Mexican beauty Salma Hayek downplayed her looks to portray the unibrowed artist Frida Kahlo, Madonna campaigned hard to win the role of the First Lady of Argentina, and Jennifer Lopez made a name for herself starring as the slain Tejano singer Selena. If Hollywood were to make a movie of your life, who should play you?

CHAPTER 16

Fried _____ Tomatoes

A Fill-in-the-Blank / Multiple Choice Pop Quiz

Y ou know them, you love them, but how much do you remember after watching them? Take a few minutes to take this chick flicks pop quiz. Answers at the end of the chapter.

Category: The Real World

1. Fill in the name of the actress who played the title role in the following big screen biographies of famous songbirds:

   a. _____ plays Loretta Lynn in *Coal Miner's Daughter* (1980).

   b. _____ plays the late country star Patsy Cline in *Sweet Dreams* (1985).

   c. _____ plays the mini-skirted half of Ike and Tina Turner in *What's Love Got to Do with It* (1993).

d. _____ plays the legendary jazz singer Billie
       Holiday (a.k.a. Lady Day) in *Lady Sings the Blues* (1972).

2. Match the popular real New York eatery with the screen lovers
   who dine there.

    1. Serendipity 3

    2. Rainbow Room

    3. Katz's Deli

    4. Tavern on the Green

    a. Meg Ryan and Billy Crystal in *When Harry Met Sally . . .*
      (1989)

    b. Meg Ryan and Bill Pullman in *Sleepless in Seattle* (1993)

    c. Meryl Streep and Jack Nicholson in *Heartburn* (1986)

    d. John Cusack and Kate Beckinsale in *Serendipity* (2001)

3. Rosalind Russell plays a nun in *The Trouble with Angels* (1966) and
   its sequel *Where Angels Go, Trouble Follows* (1968), and Whoopi
   Goldberg also dons the habit for *Sister Act* (1992) and *Sister Act 2:*
   Back in the Habit (1993). Which of the actresses headed to Fort
   Lauderdale for spring break in *Where the Boys Are* (1960) shortly
   thereafter left Hollywood to take holy vows and is still cloistered
   to this day? Hint: She also co-stars in the Montgomery Clift
   advice columnist flick *Lonelyhearts* (1958) and two of Elvis
   Presley's best vehicles, *Loving You* (1957) and *King Creole* (1958).

    a. Yvette Mimieux

    b. Connie Francis

c. Paula Prentiss

d. Dolores Hart

4. The late Frances Farmer isn't so well-known nowadays, but
    Jessica Lange's portrayal of the institutionalized actress in the film
    Frances (1982) has made her a cult figure. Name the rock star
    turned actress who married her rock star husband while wearing
    one of Frances Farmer's dresses. Hint: She later named her
    daughter Frances Bean.

Category: A Star Is Born

5. Audrey Hepburn and Katherine Hepburn were not related, but
    they did both act with the same leading men. Who of the following
    was *not* in a film with both women?

    a. Cary Grant

    b. Humphrey Bogart

    c. James Stewart

    d. Peter O'Toole

6. Many chick flick stars come from acting families. How are the
    following actors and actresses related?

    a. Isabella Rossellini, star of *Cousins* (1989) and Ingrid Bergman,
        star of *Anastasia* (1956)

    b. Angelina Jolie, star of *Girl, Interrupted* (1999) and Jon Voight,
        star of *Desert Bloom* (1986)

c. Blythe Danner, star of *The Prince of Tides* (1991) and Gwyneth Paltrow, star of *View from the Top* (2003)

   d. Melanie Griffith, star of *Working Girl* (1988) and Tippi Hedren, star of *Marnie* (1964)

   e. Joel Grey, star of *Cabaret* (1972) and Jennifer Grey, star of *Dirty Dancing* (1987)

   f. Goldie Hawn, star of *Butterflies Are Free* (1972) and Kate Hudson, star of *Raising Helen* (2004)

   g. Bridget Fonda, star of *Scandal* (1989) and Peter Fonda, star of *Tammy and the Doctor* (1963)

   h. Henry Fonda, star of *The Lady Eve* (1941) and Jane Fonda, star of *Stanley & Iris* (1990)

7. In her 1981 debut film, *Rich and Famous*, whose daughter does Meg Ryan portray?

   a. Shirley MacLaine

   b. Goldie Hawn

   c. Diane Keaton

   d. Candice Bergen

8. Who plays Jennifer Lopez's papa in *Selena* (1997)?

   a. Edward James Olmos

   b. Antonio Banderas

   c. James Gandolfini

   d. Andy Garcia

9. Name the father/daughter team who star in *Paper Moon* (1973). Bonus question: Which one won an Oscar for his or her performance?

Category: Working Girls, Part 1

10. Name the actresses whose job title is "happy hooker" in the following pictures:

   a. *Pretty Woman* (1990)

   b. *Belle de Jour* (1967)

   c. *Klute (1971)*

   d. *Dangerous Beauty* (1998)

   e. *Never on Sunday* (1960)

   f. *Moulin Rouge* (2001)

   g. *Butterfield 8* (1960)

   h. *Irma la Douce* (1963)

   i. *Back Roads* (1981)

   j. *Gigi* (1958)

   k. *Nuts* (1987)

   l. *The World of Suzie Wong* (1960)

Category: Working Girls, Part 2

11. Name the actresses who punch the clock as waitresses in the following pictures:

    a. *Alice Doesn't Live Here Anymore* (1974)

    b. *Atlantic City* (1981)

    c. *Frankie and Johnny* (1991)

    d. *Untamed Heart* (1993)

    e. *Return to Me* (2000)

    f. *Thelma & Louise* (1991)

    g. *The Wedding Singer* (1998)

    h. *White Palace* (1990)

    i. *It Could Happen to You* (1994)

    j. *Amélie* (2001)

    k. *As Good as It Gets* (1997)

12. In *How to Lose a Guy in 10 Days* (2003), Kate Hudson is writing the titular article for what fictitious magazine?

    a. *Lucky Stars*

    b. *Composure*

    c. *For Her*

    d. *Dare*

13. In *Notting Hill* (1999), Julia Roberts plays an American superstar doing publicity in London for what fictitious sci-fi motion picture?

    a. Saturn 3

    b. Helix

    c. Destination Moon

    d. AstroMom

14. *Soapdish* (1991) is a comedy focusing on the behind-the-scenes activity at what fictitious daytime soap opera?

    a. The Sun Also Sets

    b. Central Hospital

    c. Pasadena

    d. As the Days Turn

15. In *Suspect* (1987), Cher is a public defender who receives unsolicited assistance from juror Dennis Quaid. Who plays her client?

    a. Sam Shepard

    b. Liam Neeson

    c. Aidan Quinn

    d. Jason Patric

16. In *Bed of Roses* (1996), Christian Slater woos high-powered investment banker Mary Stuart Masterson by doing what?

    a. Sending her provocative e-mails.

    b. Sending her a box of Godiva chocolates.

    c. Sending her a bouquet of flowers.

    d. All of the above.

17. In *The Mirror Has Two Faces* (1996), Barbra Streisand and her husband, Jeff Bridges, share the same profession. What is it?

    a. lawyer

    b. doctor

    c. chef

    d. professor

18. In *Romy and Michele's High School Reunion* (1997), the two dumb blondes go to their ten-year reunion claiming to have invented
    _____.

Category: The Truth about Cats and Dogs

19. In which of the following movies is the lead character a single woman with a cat?

    a. *Breakfast at Tiffany's* (1961)

    b. *Bell Book and Candle* (1958)

    c. *That Darn Cat!* (1965)

    d. All of the above

20. In *Legally Blonde* (2001), what's the name of Reese Witherspoon's fashionable pooch?

    a. Pinky

    b. Tiny

    c. Tinkerbell

    d. Bruiser

Category: Details

21. In *Stepmom* (1998), Julia Roberts offers to take her stepdaughter-to-be to a concert (on a school night!) featuring which band?

    a   Nirvana

    b. Pearl Jam

    c. U2

    d. The Rolling Stones

22. In *Clueless* (1995), Alicia Silverstone's character announces that she and her best friend are named after popular singers from the past who have since done infomercials. Alicia's character is named Cher. What's her best friend's moniker?

    a. Aretha

    b. Diana

    c. Dionne

    d. Petula

23. In the *Gentlemen Prefer Blondes* (1953) production number "Diamonds Are a Girl's Best Friend," which famous gem merchant is mentioned by name?

    a. Harry Winston

    b. Cartier

    c. Tiffany

    d. All of the above

24. In *Indecent Proposal* (1993), Woody Harrelson gives away the million dollars Robert Redford paid him for one night with Demi Moore by making an outrageous bid for what animal during a charity auction?

    a. A white snow owl

    b. A spider monkey

    c. A hippo

    d. A baby elephant

Category: Titles

25. Fill in the blanks in the following titles:

    a. *To _____ on her _____ Birthday* (1996)

    b. *Captain Corelli's _____* (2001)

    c. *_____ in New York* (1963) / *_____ in New York* (2000)

d. *The Effect of* _____ _____ *on Man-in-the-Moon Marigolds* (1972)

e. *Bob &* _____ *&* _____ *& Alice* (1969)

f. *Please Don't Eat the* _____ (1960)

g. *The* _____ *of Eddie's* _____ (1963)

h. _____ *in Babysitting* (1987)

i. *For* _____ *of the Game* (1999)

j. *Every Girl Should be* _____ (1948)

k. _____ *Irresistible* (1999)

l. *Flower* _____ *Song* (1961)

m. *Looking for Mr.* _____ (1977)

n. *How to make an American* _____ (1995)

o. *The Deep End of the* _____ (1999)

p. _____ *Valentine* (1989)

q. *Save the Last* _____ (2001)

r. _____ *from the Edge* (1990)

s. *Barefoot in the* _____ (1967)

t. *Send Me No* _____ (1964)

u. _____ *Everlasting* (2002)

v. *With Six You Get* _____ (1968)

w. _____ *Gigolo* (1980)

x. *Eyes of _____ Mars* (1978)

y. *Wide _____ Sea* (1993)

z. *_____ with a Whip* (1964)

Answers:

1: a—Sissy Spacek; b—Jessica Lange; c—Angela Bassett; d—Diana Ross.

2: 1—d; 2—b; 3—a; 4—c.

3: d.

4: Courtney Love.

5: c.

6: a—daughter/mother; b—daughter/father; c—mother/daughter; d—daughter/mother; e—father/daughter; f—mother/daughter; g—daughter/father; h—father/daughter

7: d.

8: a.

9: Ryan and Tatum O'Neal. Bonus question: Tatum.

10: a—Julia Roberts; b—Catherine Deneuve; c—Jane Fonda; d—Catherine McCormack; e—Melina Mercouri; f—Nicole Kidman; g—Elizabeth Taylor; h—Shirley MacLaine; i—Sally Field; j—Leslie Caron; k—Barbra Streisand; l—Nancy Kwan.

11: a—Ellen Burstyn; b—Susan Sarandon; c—Michelle Pfeiffer; d—Marisa Tomei (and Rosie Perez as her best friend/co-worker);

e—Minnie Driver; f—Susan Sarandon (again); g—Drew Barrymore; h—Susan Sarandon (going for the triple crown of waitress performances); i—Bridget Fonda; j—Audrey Tautou; k—Helen Hunt.

12: b.

13: b.

14: a.

15: b.

16: c.

17: d.

18: Post-its.

19: d.

20: d.

21: b.

22: c.

23: d.

24: c.

25: a—Gillian, 37th; b—Mandolin; c—Sunday, Autumn; d—Gamma Rays; e—Carol, Ted; f—Daisies; g—Courtship, Father; h—Adventures; i—Love; j—Married; k—Simply; l—Drum; m—Goodbar; n—Quilt; o—Ocean; p—Shirley; q—Dance; r—Postcards; s—Park; t—Flowers; u—Tuck; v—Eggroll; w—American; x—Laura; y—Sargasso; z—Kitten.

If you got at least 50 percent correct, you can consider yourself a certified chick flick expert. Reward yourself by whipping up a celebratory batch of the ultimate chick flick gourmet treat.

FRIED GREEN TOMATOES

Served Hot

5 medium green tomatoes
1 cup self-rising cornmeal
1 cup self-rising flour
⅓ teaspoon salt
¼ teaspoon black pepper
1 cup buttermilk
Vegetable oil

Slice tomatoes into ¼-inch slices and set aside. Combine cornmeal, flour, salt, and pepper in a shallow dish. Pour buttermilk into a large bowl and add some of the tomato slices, being careful not to stack. Remove coated slices from bowl, allowing excess buttermilk to run off. Dip slices into cornmeal mixture. Repeat until all slices are coated in cornmeal. Fry in half inch of hot oil until brown, turning once to brown other side. Place in a colander to drain. As you know from the movie, fried green tomatoes have to be served hot!

CHAPTER 17

Chicks' Picks

*Reel Chicks and Real Chicks
Reveal Their Guilty Pleasures*

E ager for more? When it comes to getting additional recommendations, you can always count on your fellow chick flick enthusiasts
to share their guilty pleasures. If you're looking for a sure thing,
you can trust these chicks, both reel and real.

Reel Chicks

Fictional chicks in chick flicks watch chick flicks just like real chicks do.
Here are some of their viewing selections.

- *Romy and Michele, roommates'*:
  Pretty Woman (1990)

---

[1] *Romy and Michele's High School Reunion* (1997)

199

- *Vivian, a prostitute[2]:*
  Charade (1963)

- *Annie, a newspaper reporter[3]:*
  An Affair to Remember (1957)

- *Roberta, a housewife[4]:*
  Rebecca (1940)

- *Melanie, an architect[5]:*
  The Wizard of Oz (1939)

- *Sally, a journalist[6]:*
  Casablanca (1942)

- *Jenna, a fashion magazine editor[7]:*
  From Here to Eternity (1953)

- *Donna, a flight attendant[8]:*
  Ghost (1990)

- *Robin, a real estate agent[9]:*
  An Officer and a Gentleman (1982)
  The Way We Were (1973)

Real chicks

When one is compiling the ultimate guide to chick flicks, it's amazing how many people will offer up unexpected faves. Here are some trusty

---

[2] *Pretty Woman* (1990)   [3] *Sleepless in Seattle* (1993)   [4] *Desperately Seeking Susan* (1985)
[5] *One Fine Day* (1996)   [6] *When Harry Met Sally . . .*(1989)]   [7] *13 Going on 30* (2004)
[8] *View from the Top* (2003)   [9] *Boys on the Side* (1995)

favorites not mentioned elsewhere in this guide, complete with the chicks flick enthusiast's own editorial comments.

Maria, a television writer and screenwriter: I used the criteria that: 1. I either owned a video or DVD of the film itself to view any time the urge so hits me, or . . . 2. When channel-surfing, if I come across any of these films I ALWAYS stop to watch them, no matter what point in the movie it's at or what other favorite show I might be missing. And . . . 3. My husband, if he catches me watching, usually hangs around the TV room to tease and ridicule me for being such a girly girl.

- *Elephant Walk* (1954)—The ultimate romance novel put to film. Liz Taylor marries a rich tea plantation owner with an accent, who of course completely changes into a brooding workaholic once they get to his family estate in then-Ceylon. As he becomes more of a big drag to be with, Liz almost falls for the bad-boy foreman of the place . . . only to have pissed-off pachyderms trample the whole shebang in the third act. But there's a happy ending: True love snaps the hunky hubby out of his funk and he rescues her (and their relationship) from the ruins.

- *The Year of Living Dangerously* (1983)—A little cerebral for the category, but Mel and Sigourney's walk in the rain is one of the sexiest moments in chick flick celluloid history.

- Any Elvis movie—Need I say more?

Jonathan & Rachel, brother and sister:

- *Anne of Green Gables* (1985) and *Anne of Avonlea* (1987)

- *Empire Records* (1995)

- *Sleeping Beauty* (1959)

- *Splendor* (1999)

- *Party Girl* (1995)

- *Singles* (1992)

- *The Last Days of Disco* (1998) (whether it is a chick flick or not is arguable)

- *The Secret Garden* (1993)

- *Stealing Beauty* (1996)

- *Walking and Talking* (1996)

Cathy, a social worker and new mom:

Mr. Mom (1983)—I can't tell you how many times I've watched that movie . . . before baby was born.

The Player (1992)—I particularly like when they go to Two Bunch Palms.

Broadcast News (1987)—I have watched this way too many times.

Little House on the Prairie (1974)—I'm also a sucker for this old television show, now available on DVD.

Tootsie (1982)—A great movie.

Nicole, a chick photographer:

My #1 guilty pleasure . . . *The Legend of Billie Jean* (1985)

Kelley, a makeup artist:

Me Myself I (1999)—with Rachel Griffiths, a great film.

Julia, an editor

TV:

Sweet Hostage (1975)

The Girl Most Likely To . . . (1973)

Just One of the Guys (1985)

Theatrical Releases:

The Other Side of the Mountain (1975)

What Ever Happened to Baby Jane? (1962)

Dark Victory (1939)

Dead Ringer (1964) (with Bette Davis)

Hush . . . Hush, Sweet Charlotte (1964)

Katie, an elementary school teacher:

Heroic Women:

Julia (1977)

Aliens (1986)

Innocent Women Wise Up:

The Heiress (1949)

Great Girls and Terrific Teens:

A Tree Grows in Brooklyn (1945)

The World of Henry Orient (1964)

The Moon-Spinners (1964) (bad movie, but I love Hayley Mills)

Food:

Babette's Feast (1987)

Passionate Women:

Random Harvest (1942)

Carol, a high school teacher:

**Newer:

Norma Rae (1979)

Heaven Can Wait (1978) (W. Beatty)

Cyrano de Bergerac (1990) (G. Depardieu)

**Older:

Broken Blossoms (1919) (silent, Lillian Gish)

Sayonara (1957)

My Favorite Wife (1940) (I. Dunne, C. Grant)

Light in the Piazza (1962) (O. de Havilland)

Leslie, a Journalist:

My Guilty Pleasures (and some damn fine films):

Chasing Amy (1997)—I don't know what happened to Kevin Smith, but this is a great, funny, romantic movie.

Some Girls (1988)—Three sisters (or maybe four) go after the same guy, comic mayhem ensues. Not a lot of people know this movie, but it's definitely worth checking out.

The Sure Thing (1985)—whatever happened to Daphne Zuniga?

Tricia, a creative director in music publishing:

Superstar (1999)

Pamela, a music publisher:

My Man Godfrey (1936)

The Tenth Victim (1965)

Ariane, an artistic welder, indie-film buff:

Dark Blue World (2001)

Carrington (1995)

Dreaming of Joseph Lees (1999)

Jamie, an executive assistant:

Amy's Orgasm (2001)

I'm with Lucy (2002)

The Sweetest Thing (2002)

Juliana, a singer-songwriter/production chick:

Kill Bill Vol. 1 (2003)—Scene 1 playing with the concepts of killers with maternal instincts messed me up for quite a while . . . Uma and Viveca kicked major booty . . . great chick flick with a variety of chicks to trip on . . . Lucy Liu holding a dude's head in hand for calling her a bitch?!? If this isn't the new chick flick, what is?

Kill Bill Vol. 2 (2004)—A fine resolution.

Lara Croft: Tomb Raider (2001)—I'm glad they got Angelina J. to stand in for me, since I was too BUSY to play Lara Croft myself :-) Love her look in this flick . . . boy I sound shallow right now . . . don't remember any plot and don't care!

Carmen Jones (1954) (classic film with Harry Belafonte and Dorothy Dandridge), *The Seven Year Itch* (1955) (or any fun Marilyn Monroe flick), *Singin' in the Rain* (1952), *West Side Story . . . (1961)*, Carmen J is a classic film in the most classic, musical love story way . . . Dorothy and Harry were HOT back then looking at that flick. Mentioned Marilyn, Gene Kelly and the West Side joint all together because they're classic, old films that still move the chick in me.

Joanne & Beth, sisters:

100 Girls (2000)

Kim, a film writer: I've got a few that I know definitely qualify as chick flicks, but some of them simply feature chicks (teens, schoolgirls), so I'm not sure if they really qualify as "chick flicks" exactly. Most of them fall into the coming-of-age genre. Anyway, these are some of my favorites (in no particular order):

Secret Places (1984) d. Zelda Barron—Schoolgirls in wartime Britain; coming-of-age.

Show Me Love (1998) d. Lukas Moodysson—Girls fall in love with each other in boring Swedish town.

Times Square (1980) d. Allan Moyle—Great soundtrack; latent lesbian film set in gritty NYC.

Shag (1989) d. Zelda Barron—Southern girls go wild on Spring Break in 1960s Myrtle Beach.

Strike! (1998) d. Sarah Kernochan—Schoolgirls want to prevent their school from going coed.

L'eau Froide (1994) d. Olivier Assayas—This film is impossible to find on video, but it's one of the best youth-centric films ever.

Emporte-Moi (Set Me Free) (1999) d. Léa Pool—A tribute to the French New Wave from a girl's POV.

Sister My Sister (1994) d. Nancy Meckler—True crime in the vein of *Heavenly Creatures*.

How to Deal (2003) d. Clare Kilner—I'm kind of embarrassed to admit it, but I really liked this movie.

Cecil, a children's book author:

A Matter of Life and Death (1946)

Secretary (2002)

I Know Where I'm Going! (1945)

Me Without You (2001)

The Princess and the Warrior (2000)

The Truth about Cats and Dogs (1996)

Camille Claudel (1989)

Harold and Maude (1971)

Il Postino (1994)

Groundhog Day (1993)

The African Queen (1951)

Girlfight (2000)

My Beautiful Laundrette (1985)

L.A. Story (1991)

Robin and Marian (1976)

Housesitter (1992)

Eternal Sunshine of the Spotless Mind (2004)

Only the Lonely (1991)

Siesta (1987)

Lynn, a film director's assistant:

Beyond the Valley of the Dolls (1970)

Black Mama, White Mama (1972)

Desperate Teenage Lovedolls (1984)

Smithereens (1982)

Double Happiness (1994)

Eve's Bayou (1997)

Flirt (1995) (Hal Hartley)

Flirting (1991) (John Duigan—featuring a young Nicole Kidman)

Gregory's Girl (1981)

Ladies and Gentlemen, the Fabulous Stains (1981) (featuring a young Diane Lane)

Mi Vida Loca (1994)

Women on the Verge of a Nervous Breakdown (1988)

and from the Keanu collection:

Point Break (1991)

Kate, a D-Girl:

Any Russ Meyers movie

Labyrinth (1986)

Whale Rider (2003)

Written on the Wind (1956)

Molly-Dodd, a corporate executive:

Indochine (1992)

Badlands (1973)

The Heart Is a Lonely Hunter (1968)

Dinner at Eight (1933)

Kitty Foyle (1940)

The Thomas Crown Affair (1999) (new one)

Where the Heart Is (2000)

The Graduate (1967)

Rear Window (1954)

Diva (1982)

Local Hero (1983)

Roseanna's Grave (1997)

Intern (2000)

To Kill a Mockingbird (1962) (is this a chick flick?)

Defending Your Life (1991)

A Streetcar Named Desire (1951)

Carol, a screenwriter:

Once Around (1991) (Richard Dreyfuss and Holly Hunter) A little-seen tearjerker.

Dear Heart (1964) (Glenn Ford and Geraldine Page)—Possibly the best love story ever set at a post office convention. The perfect rental for Glenn Ford fans and mail carriers alike.

Fame (1980)—That scene where they dance on the cars makes the whole movie worth watching.

Lost in Translation (2003)—Surprisingly, in 2003, along comes a movie with true romantic tension; maybe there's hope for the future of love stories after all.

Notes

Page

2 **"It has been said . . ."** "Chick Flicks: Amy Pascal of Columbia Pictures," *Los Angeles Magazine*, August 2001.

2 **"I don't like the term"** Nina Garin, "While women tend to flock to a 'chick flick,' most men flee the coop," *Union-Tribune*, December 19, 2003.

8 **"Love is the ultimate magic,"** *Practical Magic* Original Theatrical Release Press Kit, Warner Bros., 1998, p. 11.

9 **"Invariably the 'third character' part . . ."** *Two Weeks Notice* Original Theatrical Release Press Kit, Warner Bros., 2002, p. 6.

9 **"Dennis made Eddie . . ."** *Something to Talk About* Original Theatrical Release Press Kit, Warner Bros., 1995, p. 4.

9 **"Tom has such charm,"** *You've Got Mail* Original Theatrical Release Press Kit, Warner Bros., 1998, p. 5.

11 **"We all have certain questions . . ."** *Crossroads* Original Theatrical Release Press Kit, Paramount Pictures and Zomba Films, 2002, p. 7.

11 **"Walter represents the perfect . . ."** *Sleepless in Seattle* Original Theatrical Release Press Kit, Tri-Star Pictures, Inc., 1993, p. 6.

12 **"I know the world . . ."** *Bridget Jones's Diary* Original Theatrical Release Press Kit, A Miramax Films Release, 2001, p. 6.

12 **"They have this kind of chance meeting,"** *The Wedding Planner* Original Theatrical Release Press Kit, Columbia Pictures Industries, Inc, 2001, p. 6.

13 **"I think the most incredible . . ."** *The Wedding Singer* Original Theatrical Release Press Kit, New Line Cinema, 1998, p. 3.

13   **"The trap in making romantic . . ."** *Sweet Home Alabama* Original Theatrical Release Press Kit, Touchstone Pictures, 2002, p. 10.

14   **"I tried to make this film . . ."** *Sweet November* Original Theatrical Release Press Kit, Warner Bros. Pictures and Bel-Air Pictures, LLC, 2001, p. 7.

14   **"We think of it as . . ."** *The Wedding Planner* Press Kit, p. 9.

15   **"awwwwww"** and **"I wish that were meeeeeeee!"** Internet Posting by Mandy Koch, July 16, 2003.

20   **"every single moment that . . ."** *Titanic* Original Theatrical Release Press Kit, Twentieth Century Fox, 1997, p. 8.

20   **"I believe this story . . ."** *Ibid.*

20   **"We wanted to tell a . . ."** *Ibid.*

21   **"in essence but not in particular"** *How Stella Got Her Groove Back* Original Theatrical Release Press Kit, Twentieth Century Fox, 1998, p. 5.

22   **"I was standing in the restroom . . ."** *Romy and Michele's High School Reunion* Original Theatrical Release Press Kit, Touchstone Pictures, 1997, p. 6.

22   **"I had to add further . . ."** *Ibid.*

22   **"We thought: what kind . . ."** *The Wedding Planner* Press Kit, New Line Cinema, 1998, p. 3

23   **"What we found out . . ."** *Ibid.*

23   **"Two Women, Three Men, One Secret."** *The Favor* Original Theatrical Release Press Kit Orion Pictures, 1994, p. 1.

23   **"Please look up my . . ."** *Ibid.*, p. 3.

24   **"When I was lying . . ."** *Notting Hill* Original Theatrical Release Press Kit, Universal Pictures, 1999, pp. 8–9.

24   **"People will just assume . . ."** *Ibid.*, p. 10.

25   **"I was having a spectacularly . . ."** *One Fine Day* Original Theatrical Release Press Kit Twentieth Century Fox, 1996, p. 2.

25   **"I'm always drawn . . ."** *Ibid.*

28   **"There's a dearth of good . . ."** *Emma* Original Theatrical Release Press Kit, A Miramax Films Release, 1996, p. 3.

29   **"The question I asked myself . . ."** *Sabrina* Original Theatrical Release Press Kit, Paramount Pictures Corporation, 1995, p. 7.

29   **"Julia Ormand has . . ."** *Ibid.*

30   **"I knew that . . ."** *City of Angels* Original Theatrical Release Press Kit, Warner Brothers Productions LTD./Monarchy Enterprises B.V./Regency Entertainment, 1998, p. 9.

35   **"The common bond that . . ."** *The Wedding Singer* Press Kit, p. 8

36   **"The road in this film . . ."** *Boys on the Side* Original Theatrical Release Press Kit, Monarchy Enterprises, C.V. and Le Studio Canal+, 1995, p. 7.

36   **"Carrie is a very modern . . ."** *Four Weddings and a Funeral* Original Theatrical Release Press Kit, MGM/UA, 1994, p. 3.

37   **"Vianne is a wanderer . . ."** *Chocolat* Original Theatrical Release Press Kit, A Miramax Films Release, 2000, p. 15.

38   **"It clearly affirms . . ."** *Serendipity* Original Theatrical Release Press Kit, A Miramax Release, 2001, p. 20.

39   **"[The former Columbia studio head] Dawn Steel . . ."** *While You Were Sleeping* Original Theatrical Release Press Kit, Hollywood Pictures, 1995, p. 12.

39   **"I felt that Hope Floats . . ."** *Hope Floats* Original Theatrical Release Press Kit, Twentieth Century Fox, 1998, p. 1.

40   **"It's about starting over . . ."** *Ibid.*

40   **"I think every young girl . . ."** *What a Girl Wants* Original Theatrical Release Press Kit, Warner Bros. Pictures, 2003, p. 2.

40   **"Maggie has run away . . ."** *Runaway Bride* Original Theatrical Release Press Kit, Paramount Pictures, 1996, p. 8.

41   **"At the beginning . . ."** *Ibid.*

41   **"Everybody has a moment . . ."** *Legally Blonde* Original Theatrical Release Press Kit, Metro-Goldwyn-Mayer, 2001, p. 4.

43   **"I love Drew"** *The Wedding Singer* Press Kit, p. 3.

44   **"has an innate connection . . ."** *Mona Lisa Smile* Press Kit, p. 14.

44   **"I was fascinated . . ."** *Ibid.*, p. 18.

46   **"I think Tom . . ."** *You've Got Mail* Original Theatrical Release Press Kit, Warner Bros., 1998, p. 5.

47   **"People might look . . ."** *Two Weeks Notice* Press Kit, p. 3.

49   **"When I signed on . . ."** *The Wedding Planner* Press Kit, p. 5.

57   **"To find just the right . . ."** *Two Weeks Notice* Press Kit, p. 3.

57   **"We chose Aidan . . ."** *Practical Magic* Press Kit, p. 5.

57   **"He was adorable."** *The Favor* Press Kit, p. 8.

58   **"Trip had to be . . ."** *The Virgin Suicides* Original Theatrical Release Press Kit, Paramount Classics, 2000, p. 13.

58   **"When [director] Lewis Gilbert . . ."** *Educating Rita* Original Theatrical Release Press Kit, Columbia Pictures, 1983, p. 1.

58   **"The story has to . . ."** *What Women Want* Original Theatrical Release Press Kit, Paramount Pictures, 2000, p. 5.

59   **"All you have to be . . ."** *Ibid.*, p. 6.

61 **"But then when I . . ."** *Pride and Prejudice* DVD liner notes, BBC Television and A& E Entertainment, 2001.

61 **"I think he's actually . . ."** *Bridget Jones's Diary* Press Kit, p. 8.

63 **Director Michael Hoffman cites,** *One Fine Day* Original Theatrical Release Press Kit, Twentieth Century Fox, 1996, p. 4.

63 **"a kind of Pillow . . ."** *Ibid.*

73 **"Some whore gets to . . ."** **"Top 10 chick flicks all time, also known as my wife's favorite movies."** *www. RankOVision.com*, 2004.

84 **"Vivian is a real victim . . ."** *Pretty Woman*, Original Theatrical Release Press Kit, Touchstone Pictures, 1990, p. 14.

85 **"I think the beauty . . ."** *Ibid.*

97 **"Ballroom dancing allows anybody . . ."** *Strictly Ballroom* Original Theatrical Release Press Kit, A Miramax Release, 1992, p. 5.

102 **"The story really touches . . ."** *Amélie* Original Theatrical Release Press Kit, A Miramax Release, 2001, p. 17.

104 **"Dirty dancing is the most erotic . . ."** *Dirty Dancing* Original Theatrical Release Press Kit, Vestron Pictures, 1987, p. 11.

104 **"Dirty Dancing is like soul dancing . . ."** *Ibid.*

106 **"I'll write you a story,"** *The Princess Bride* Original Theatrical Release Press Kit, The Princess Bride Limited, 1987, p. 3.

110 **"I got the idea while . . ."** *Thelma & Louise* Original Theatrical Release Press Kit, Metro-Goldwyn-Mayer, 1991, p. 3.

110 **"As a person, I . . ."** *Ibid.*

115 **"Surgery took years . . ."** *Ash Wednesday* VHS video box cover, copyright ©1973 Paramount Pictures and Sagittarius Productions, Inc.

116 **"The rules of the dogfight"** *Dogfight* VHS video box cover, copyright ©1991 Warner Bros.

119 **"They love Paris . . ."** *A New Kind of Love* VHS video box cover, copyright ©1963 Paramount Pictures.

120 **"A story about husbands . . ."** *Something to Talk About* VHS video box cover, copyright ©1996 Paramount Pictures.

170 **"the movie starts out . . ."** *A Walk to Remember* Original Theatrical Release Press Kit, copyright ©2002 Pandora, Inc., p. 10.

175 **"Ridiculed for her clothes . . ."** *Stella Dallas* Original Theatrical Placard, copyright ©1937, United Artists.

200 **Real chicks:** All recommended viewing lists contributed by identified real chicks via email correspondence, February–April, 2004.

Photo Credits

13 Charlize Theron and Keanu Reeves star in Warner Bros. Pictures' and Bel-Air Entertainment's romantic drama *Sweet November*. Copyright© 2001 Warner Bros. Pictures and Bel-Air Pictures, LLC. Photographer: Merie W. Wallace.

14 Jennifer Lopez and Matthew McConaughey star as a couple who find love at a very inconvenient time in the charming Columbia Pictures romantic comedy *The Wedding Planner*. Copyright © 2001 Columbia Pictures Industries, Inc. Photographer: Ron Batzdorff.

15 Daniel Day-Lewis and Madeline Stowe star in *The Last of the Mohicans*. Copyright © 1992 Warner Bros., © 1992 Morgan Creek International, Inc.

16 Tom Cruise and Renée Zellweger star in *Jerry Mcguire*. Copyright © 1996 TriStar Pictures, Inc.

17 James Stewart, Cary Grant, and Katherine Hepburn in *The Philadelphia Story*, a Metro-Goldwyn-Mayer Picture. Copyright © 1940, Metro-Goldwyn-Mayer.

18 Mae Whitman as Maggie, George Clooney as Jack, Michelle Pfeiffer as Melanie, and Alex D. Linz as Sammy share a frantic cab ride in *One Fine Day*. Copyright © 1996 Twentieth Century Fox. Photographer: Gemma LaMana.

23 Ken Wahl portrays Tom Andrews, Bill Pullman is Peter Whiting, and Brad Pitt portrays Elliot Fowler in the Orion Pictures' romantic comedy *The Favor*. Copyright © 1994 Orion Pictures. Photographer: Lorey Sebastian.

26 Alicia Silverstone stars as Cher in *Clueless*. Copyright © 1995 Paramount Pictures.

30 Academy Award winner Nicolas Cage stars with Meg Ryan in *City of Angels*, a story of romance and desire from Warner Bros. in association with Regency Pictures and Atlas Entertainment. Copyright © 1998 Warner Brothers Productions LTD./Monarchy Enterprises B.V./Regency Entertainment (U.S.A.).

34 Whoopi Goldberg, Mary-Louise Parker, and Drew Barrymore in Warner Bros.' *Boys on the Side*. Copyright © 1995 Monarchy Enterprises, C.V., and Le Studio Canal+. Photographer: Suzanne Hanover.

38 Kate Beckinsale and John Cusack in Peter Cheslom's *Serendipity*. A Miramax Release Copyright ©2001. Photographer: David Lee.

43 Julia Roberts as the title character in *Runaway Bride*. Copyright © 1996 Paramount Pictures.

44 Kat Arujo (Annabeth Gish) and her sister, Daisy (Julia Roberts), collide in the Mystic Pizza Parlor, where they are waitresses in *Mystic Pizza*, a Samuel Goldwyn Company presentation. Copyright © 1988 The Samuel Goldwyn Company. Photographer: Paul Slaughter.

46 Determined to marry a genius like her uncle Albert Einstein, Catherine Boyd (Meg Ryan) is engaged to James Moreland (Stephen Fry) in *I.Q.* Copyright © 1994 Paramount Pictures. Photographer: Demmie Todd.

47 Sandra Bullock stars as an unrefined FBI agent who goes undercover as a contestant in a beauty pageant, along with Michael Caine and Benjamin Bratt, in *Miss Congeniality*, a Castle Rock Entertainment production in association with Village Roadshow of a Warner Bros. Pictures release. Copyright © 2000 Castle Rock Entertainment. Photographer: Ron Batzdorff.

49 Selena (Jennifer Lopez) and Chris Lopez (Jon Seda) in *Selena*. Copyright © 1997 Warner Bros. Photographer: Scott Del Amo.

51 Drew Barrymore as Danielle in *Ever After*. Copyright © 1998 Twentieth Century Fox.

52 Gwyneth Paltrow portrays the wealthy and beautiful Estella in *Great Expectations*. Copyright © 1997 Twentieth Century Fox. Photographer: Phillip Caruso.

53 Reese Witherspoon as Elle Woods in *Legally Blonde*. Copyright © 2001 Metro-Goldwyn-Mayer. Photographer: Tracy Bennett.

54 Audrey Hepburn in William Wyler's production of *Roman Holiday*. Copyright © 1953 Paramount Pictures Corporation.

56 Colin Firth and Hugh Grant in Sharon Maguire's *Bridget Jones's Diary*. A Miramax Films Release Copyright © 2001. Photographer: Alex Bailey.

59 The Prime Minister (Hugh Grant) and Natalie (Martine McCutcheon) are caught off-guard (and quite by accident) at a Christmas pageant in Richard Curtis's romantic comedy *Love Actually*. Copyright © 2003 Universal Studios. Photographer: Peter Mountain

61 Colin Firth plays Amanda Bynes's father in *What a Girl Wants*. Copyright © 2003 Warner Bros. Pictures, an AOL Time Warner Company. Photographer: Frank Connor.

62 Jack Taylor (George Clooney) and his daughter Maggie (Mae Whitman) find a rare moment of relaxation during one very hectic day in *One Fine Day*. Copyright © 1996 Twentieth Century Fox. Photo: Myles Aronwitz.

63 Brad Pitt in *Interview with the Vampire: The Vampire Chronicles*. Copyright © 1994 Warner Bros.

65 Nicolas Cage in *Moonstruck*. Copyright © 1987 Metro-Goldwyn-Mayer Pictures, Inc.

66 Lloyd Dobler (John Cusack), a young nonconformist, falls in love with beautiful, brilliant Diane Court (Ione Skye) in Twentieth Century Fox's *Say Anything*, an unlikely love story from the producers of *Big* and *Broadcast News* and the creator of *Fast Times at Ridgemont High*. Copyright © 1989 Twentieth Century Fox. Photographer: Gemma LaMana Wills.

67 Franka Potente and Johnny Depp star in New Line Cinema's drama *Blow*. Copyright © 2001 New Line Cinema. Photographer: L. Sebastian.

69 Ex-Secret Service agent and professional bodyguard Frank Farmer (Kevin Costner) is hired to protect glamorous actress/singer Rachel Marron (Whitney Houston) in Warner Bros.' romantic suspense-thriller *The Bodyguard*. Copyright (©1992 Warner Bros.

70 Cary Grant and Rosalind Russell with Ralph Bellamy in Howard Hawk's *His Girl Friday*. A Columbia Picture Release. Copyright © 1940.

72 Marcie Leeds and Mayim Bialik in *Beaches*. Copyright © 1988 Touchstone Pictures. All rights reserved. Photographer: Louis Goldman .

74 Robert Redford and Barbra Streisand in *The Way We Were*. Copyright © 1973 Columbia Pictures.

75 When Marianne (Kate Winslet) injures her ankle during a rainstorm, she is literally swept off her feet by Willoughby (Greg Wise) in Columbia Pictures' romantic comedy *Sense and Sensibility*. Copyright © 1995 Columbia Pictures Industries, Inc. Photographer: Clive Coote.

76 Gwyneth Paltrow as Viola and Joseph Fiennes as Will in *Shakespeare in Love*. A Miramax Films Release Copyright © 1998.

77 Hector Elizondo reads the marriage ceremony to Bette Midler and John Heard in *Beaches*. Copyright © MCMLXXXIX Touchstone Pictures. Photographer: Jane O'Neal.

78 Sally Field, Julia Roberts, Dolly Parton, Shirley MacLaine, Daryl Hannah, and Olympia Dukakis star in *Steel Magnolias*. Copyright © 1989 TriStar Pictures, Inc.

80 Annie Reed (Meg Ryan) flies across the country just to get a glimpse of a man she has only heard on a radio call-in show in the romantic comedy *Sleepless in Seattle*, a TriStar Pictures release. Copyright © 1993 TriStar Pictures, Inc.

81 Harry (Billy Crystal) proves to Sally (Meg Ryan) that he can admit he was wrong in *When Harry Met Sally* . . .Copyright © 1989 Castle Rock Entertainment.

82 Clark Gable and Vivien Leigh in *Gone with the Wind*, a David O. Selznick Technicolor Production released by Metro-Goldwyn Mayer. Copyright © 1939 Metro-Goldwyn Mayer.

83 George Peppard and Audrey Hepburn in *Breakfast at Tiffany's*. Copyright © 1961 by Paramount Pictures Corporation and Jurrow-Shepherd Production.

84 Richard Gere and Julia Roberts in *Pretty Woman*. Copyright © 1990 Touchstone Pictures.

86 Michael Douglas and Annette Bening star in *The American President* in which the chief executive falls for an environmental lobbyist. Directed by Rob Reiner,

the Castle Rock Entertainment film is a Columbia Pictures release. Copyright © 1995 Castle Rock Entertainment. Photographer: Michael O'Neill.

rich and successful businesswomen, but are soon exposed by a former class-mate in Touchstone Pictures' comedy, *Romy and Michele's High School Reunion*. Copyright © 1997 Touchstone Pictures. Photographer: Mark Fellman.

212 Anna Paquin and Rachael Leigh Cook in a scene from Robert Iscove's *She's All That*. Copyright © 1999 A Miramax Films Release. Photographer: Claudette Barius.

Acknowledgments

The author wishes to thank (in alphabetical order):

Sylvia Abumuhor
Kevin Ackerman
Molly-Dodd Wheeler
   Adams
Craig Adelman
Howard Adelman
Nancy Adelman
David Birdsell
Beth Bloom
Joanne Bloom
Natalie Bovis
Ariane Brittany
Maria Burton
Matt Cartsonis
Susan Cartsonis
Cecil Castellucci
William Clark
Pamela Coady
Becky Cole
Charles Cook
Carmen Cuba
Natasha Cuba
Beth Datlowe
Maria de la Torre
Leslie Dinaberg
Pavel Dyden

Noah Edelson
Debbie Felton
Bear Fisher
Kathleen French
Linda Gordon
Bryan Hale
Pamela Harris
Thomas Ethan Harris
Gavin Harvey
Carol Heikkinen
Tricia Holloway
Andre Jacquemetton
Maria Jacquemetton
Juliana Jai
Sara Juarez
David King
Cathy Kline
Jeff Kline
Zak Klobucher
Mandy Koch
Holly Mandel
Steve Markoff
Carol May
Andrew Mersmann
Loren Miller
Dean Minerd

Lynn Padilla
Jeff Payne
Bob Pederson
Laura Phillips
Kate Purdy
Doris Quon
Jamie Rabb
Douglas Ross
Jonathan Ruane
Rachael Ruane
Julia Rubiner
Ralph Sall
Mara Schwartz
Kimberly Sharp
Carol Sheridan
Katie Shiban
Tricia Stewart Shiu
Lesley Marlene Siegel
Greg Stewart
Peggy Van Norman
Deb Vaughan
Nicole Weingart
Craig Wells
Wendy Wilson
Alison Winward
Kimberly Yutani

223

Index of Films

© Carol Sheridan

About the Author

Kim Adelman's first job out of college was working as a studio executive's assistant at Twentieth Century Fox. Her most treasured souvenir from those days is a promotional mug for *Working Girl* that reads "There's more to life than smiling, filing and dialing." Ms. Adelman subsequently spent three years producing short films for the Fox Movie Channel. Exposed daily to the cable channel's expansive catalogue of classic women's pictures, she became a hardcore fan of chick flick director extraordinaire Jean Negulesco (*How to Marry a Millionaire*, *The Best of Everything*, *Three Coins in the Fountain*, and so many other greats). A filmmaker whose work has premiered at the prestigious Sundance Film Festival, Ms. Adelman currently teaches filmmaking and marketing at UCLA Extension. She is also the author of *The Girls' Guide to Elvis*, *The Girls' Guide to Country*, and *The Ultimate Filmmaker's Guide to Short Films*.